# A TINY but RADIANT

# LIGHT

### On the Pathway to Eternity

*One Woman's Mystical Experience—
A Revelation in the 20$^{Th}$ Century*

**Margaret Mary Stender**

**TigerEye Publications**
P.O. Box 6382
Springdale, Arkansas 72766
*www.TigerEyePubs.com*

A Tiny but Radiant Light

Copyright © 2015 by Margaret Mary Stender

All rights reserved. No portion or part of this book may be reproduced, copied or transmitted in any form, electronically or by mechanical means, including photocopying, recording or by any information storage and retrieval system without the written permission of the author.

ISBN: 978-1511913416

Printed in USA

OTHER BOOKS
BY THIS AUTHOR

Behold the Daybreak

The Greening Springing

IN APPRECIATION

To Sally Hainline, of Lawton, Michigan, for her treasured friendship and for the phenomenal cover design; to John and Ila Clements, Larry Stroud, and Ruby Fair of Batesville, Arkansas, for their encouragement and support; to one of my favorite people, my niece and editor, Kristi Edwards, and to Rick Baber, of TigerEye Publications, for his ongoing expertise and diligence in the publication of this work.

DEDICATION

To Seth,
a thoughtful, warmhearted loving human being and jovial husband,
father, grandfather, and great-grandfather,
and to Steven, the youngest.

# A TINY but RADIANT LIGHT

# TABLE OF CONTENTS

## CHAPTER I
FIRST WORDS—Awakened by a Sound as the Rushing of Winds
Mystical Revelation Revealed—An Overview..........................1

## CHAPTER II
PRELUDE—Mysticism Propounded in the Twentieth Century..........3
   Deepest, Darkest Shadow and Despair
   Fortuitous Desire—The Author's Story

## CHAPTER III
EVENING AND MOMENT—Espousal of Above and Below..........10
   Recognition of *Something,* Soon to Occur
   Thunderous Sound: The Enkindling—The Crowning
   Knowledge Known—Entwined with Thunderous Sound
     —The Enkindling
     Poetry in Affirmation of the Knowledge Known
       When Knowledge Knows Itself to Be
       The Overflowing, the Gush and Wane

## CHAPTER IV
NEW LIFE LIVING WITHIN—The Life Speaks Out in You...........22
   Calm—The Silence Under the Sound
     Poetry in Desire of the Sea of Perpetual Calm
       In Simplicity and Stillness Sat
   Laudable Presence—The Bounty of Calm
     Poetry in Celebration of the Presence Within
       The Lull
   Love Eternal—O My Virgin Sophia, O My Noble Love
     Poetry in Light of the Love
       Ignited, the Light Lives
       Love thus Tendering Encircles
   Riotous Bounteous Joy—Over-Joyousness Expounding
     Poetry in Appreciation of the Illustrious Joy
       The Warble
       O Joy, Thou Livest as a Flame
       Sounding Forth the Joy
     Poetry by Edward Carpenter, Speaks of the Joy
       Youth Within—*The Radiant Boy*
     Poetry in Delight of Vibrant Youth
       Youth Born Arising

## CHAPTER V
GENERATION—Gifts—Succeeding the Evening and Moment.......39
- The Veil is Rent
- Embodiement of Harmony

Poetry—Desire, Necessity to Express
- Wind Takes Its Rush, but Leaves Its Hush Behind

Visions—The Living Life Within the Living Life
- Poetry in Honor of the Prophetic Visions
  - Given the Fourth
  - The Sun Appeared with Motion Teeming

To Breach the Gap—You Are the Living Life within the Living Life
Golden Glow—The Wonderment
- Still Wonder Interior to All
- Bubbling Golden, as Ginger Floating

## CHAPTER VI
LOSS OF LOVE ETERNAL—Loss of Actively Living as One........68
Poetry in Outcry of the Declivity of the Colossal Love
- Eternal
- Light the Light
- For the Absence of its Lily
- Exceed within My Being
- Bleat, but for Thy Calm
- The Tiny One Affords to the Infinite

## CHAPTER VII
HEART-SOBBING DETRIMENTAL DECLINE—Ariseth Soul and Mind to God....................................................................…......75
Veneration the Second—An Impermanent Selfishness
- Poetry—Forth Arising Prayers
  - Ebbs, Swells, Leaves its High-Water Mark, then Flows
  - The Holier Defeated My Defeat
  - Truth Sustaining Truth

Meant of Creation—Life, Itself, A-Pulsing—The Blossom
- Poetry—Happy Hope to Substantial Faith
  - Once the Blossom Bursts
  - It is Time

Port of Your Return—Love Doth Seeth and Whisper
- Poetry in View of Happy Hope
  - Alert Withon the Top—Immortality
  - Opened by An Unseen Hand
  - Never the Flame to Darken Out

## CHAPTER VIII
FINAL WORDS—Rest in the Knowledge..................................89

## CHAPTER IX
LET US TAKE A SLIGHT FORK IN THE ROAD—Affinity.........94
A Trudge Along Another Path, Proceed at an Unknown Pace

## CHAPTER X
RICHARD MAURICE BUCKE, M.E.—Marks of Cosmic Sense......96
The Soul Is Triumphant
Life is Purely Life

## CHAPTER XI
JOHN MIDDLETON MURRY—"An Experience That Enabled
Me to Understand" ......................................................120

## CHAPTER XII
WALT WHITMAN—Onset of Illumination, by Virtue of Association
with Whitman........................................................................159

## CHAPTER XIII
ELSE BARKER—Written Through the Hand of, 1914................164

## CHAPTER XIV
EVENING AND MOMENT COMMENTARY:
THUNDEROUS SOUND —The Enkindling......................189

APPENDIX....................................................................194
  Poetry, Enamored of Faraway Heavenly Music
    Harken Low to Listen
    Thunderous Sound: The Enkindling—The Crowning—
      The Crux of this entire narrative, a selection from
        *Megan's Story*
  Poetry of the Sea of Perpetual Calm
    This Day Awakening Tempering
    Lull—The Crown of Pearl
  Poetry in Light of the Love
    As the Love Doth Live
    O Gentle Ennoble Man
    O Gentle Ennoble Man—Expounded
    Furbishing Forth
  Poetry in Delight of Vibrant Youth
    O Wondrous Child
    Yet You Stayed, O Loyalty

Poetry of the Hallowed Golden Glow
    Withwonderment—A Vision
    Alight the Night with Daybright
    Then Dawned the Second Birth—A Vision
    The Golden Hallowed Glow—A Vision
Poetry of the Meant of Creation
    All Flaws Abolished by the Light—A Vision
    Three Landscape Paintings—A Vision
Poetry, the Joy of Immortality
    Sea unto Ourselves
    Lull Too
    All the While—A Selection
Poetry of the Loss of the Sense of Sin
    Goes Its Way a Cautioning
    Macro Goal
Poetry to the Germination or Bud, the Blessed Rhythm
    Ever Faithful
    From Whooshing Storms to Bearing Life and Calm
ANOTHER'S MYSTICAL EXPERIENCE—Non-Poetic…...220

# CHAPTER I

## FIRST WORDS—Awakened by a Sound as the Rushing of Winds

### Mystical Revelation Revealed

#### An Overview

In July 1991, she was awakened by a sound as the rushing of winds, appearing from nowhere, tearing through the dark, and swiftly approaching: then, a kindling, a type of pulsing burst or flare within her head; a powerful traveling of its effect first up, then down and out through her arms and down her chest; an abrupt halt; a peace and tranquility ascended—emerged from her interior being—accompanied by a love and a joy surpassing description—a satiation, a physical gratification, beyond compare; a complete-absorbing calm rested with her for one full week; a mediating presence thrived full-fledged for three plus months then lasted intermittently for many years. Numerous gifts were endowed, gradually, woefully, diminishing.

This is the true story of one woman's mystical experience, perhaps ineptly told: She was blessed with the greatest of gifts: a blithe-full calm; a buoyant eternal love—Love Eternal; a knowledge etched *withon* her soul; a riotous bounteous joy; the Youth within; the Golden Glow; the prophetic visions; the 180-degree radical transition of life; and the necessity to write in a poetical vein—to expound upon, to applaud and to announce of the Gift inborn, instilled within; to alert to the wondrousness of the supernal *creation*, the region within the each of us.

## Margaret Mary Stender

Over a period of years, the gifts declined; a powerful overwhelming personal lament arose only to burrow to the depths of the soul; this cardinal loss led to a severe crisis, an enforced contradiction, nearly a delirium to regain the lost. Immersed in an inner-sobbing, there appeared a progressive pleading-in-desperate-struggle—the resultant aftermath of the mounting loss. In juxtaposition, a buoyant joy continued to arouse her upward to battle its way, inhabiting the soul, to convey it toward the eternal.

Eventually, it was apparent that the knowledge of the gifts must be shared, not merely in the substance of the inspired poetry previously published, but intentionally, candidly. Woefully, against her active will, impelled, it became essential to relate the evening's experience in concise language, and to *take a slight fork in the road* in an endeavor to correlate the various personal aspects with the spiritual experience of other individuals; albeit the other individuals are persons of renown, wherein she is purely a normal, an average, woman, born in 1938.

In intimate detail, the comparison corroborates the attributes of the endowed gifts, or openly avows the deficiency of their nature. It speaks to the elements leading to and succeeding this miraculous decisive mystical experience. This is one woman's personal story, a revelation in the 20$^{th}$ century; a mystical revelation revealed.

*Let Us Take a Slight Fork in the Road* consists of a comparison of attributes, gifts of the evening, with the marks of cosmic sense, identified by Richard Maurice Bucke, in *Cosmic Consciousness*, and with the personal illumination experience of John Middleton Murry delineated and assessed in his autobiography, titled *God*.

In August 2009, after this entire composition was in major part complete, Elsa Barker's book, *Letters from a Living Dead Man* was brought to her attention. LETTER XXXV speaks of "The Beautiful Being." A fascinating recognition is immediately perceived between the Beautiful Being and a primary gift of the evening's mystical experience; the gift of the Presence.

## CHAPTER II

## PRELUDE—Mysticism Propounded in the Twentieth Century

### Deepest, Darkest Shadow and Despair

Lo, those many years ago, 1970, sheer agony, sitting on the end of the bed attempting to break through the torment, immersed in sorrow, I slumped in quiet desperation: head hung, shoulders drooped, back slouched. I concentrated wholeheartedly in my juvenile attempt to communicate into the unknown, the vast expanse, to "find" my mother.

In December 1969, Mom died suddenly with nearly no warning. The surgeon's knife had slipped and cut a main artery down her back. She immediately went into shock from the loss of blood. In the surgeon's attempt to revive her, she aspirated inhaling the fluid and burning her lungs. After the surgery, oxygen could no longer be properly absorbed. She could no longer communicate. The local hospital transferred her to a major hospital in Ann Arbor. Although the doctors tried, they were unable to help her. She suffered arduously until her death three weeks later.

A pivotal night a few months after my mother's death, an unbearable sorrow and a dreadful despair plagued and permeated my being. Fervent intention compelled me to try now to reach her, to grasp into the beyond. I was determined. If there were a means to locate Mom, to see if she was all right, to delve into the unknown to express our family's severe life-staggering unhappiness, our dreadful heart-wrenching grief, our earnest love, I would try to find it that night.

I sat at the end of the bed in full unequivocal absorption, guided only by determination and simple conviction and attempted to focus my thoughts. Repeatedly I attempted to expand the thoughts *out* to reach her; to stretch my mind outward into space—outward into the unknown—to encompass all eternity, and inward to focus the concentration, to eliminate all other thought; to incorporate the *all*. Determination was staunch, unshakable, albeit, there was a placid underlying knowledge, which inherently recognized, that some form of a barrier, nearly impenetrable, would have to be breached.

Perhaps an *undeveloped* intuition also drew me to solemnity, to the quietude of this evening. I had previously read of situations regarding other persons, themselves embroiled in gloomy desperation, reaching *out* to their lost loved ones. I believed that I could not go on without her, at least without reaching her; her loss was so acute, so staunch, so severe. My father was devastated. My siblings were stunned as deeply as I. We were desolate. What were we to do?

The desperation was intense; the concentration was intense. The time where I sat at the end of the bed was so prolonged; I knew if ever I were to reach her, it would be that night. Through our love for each other, we must interconnect, somehow. What she had been through resulting in the loss of her life was unfair and unjustifiable. I knew that to go on, I must find out if she *is* all right.

(I do not recall whether on that night there was a quiet underlying understanding that to locate Mom was to also affirm an everlasting life, but in thinking back, I doubt there was that level of clear comprehension.)

In a brief instance, all consciousness of my surroundings was obliterated from mind and sight. Then jarred, as if by an unheard sound, my eyes bolted open. It was as if I had been called. Alert, I startled, and all in one motion turned my head and peered intently to the right. Aghast, I perceived my own downtrodden slumped-over reflection in the window glass against the dark backdrop of night.

The dim light of the bedroom shown around the reflection. Incredulous, perturbed at being disturbed, I stared at my own image. The miracle of absorption, or whatever silence or force that caused or allowed me to access that momentary unexplainable undeniable region, when consciousness of my surroundings was lost, was shattered as crystal. To my dismay, I was unable to retrieve it.

There was no vast discovery, no vision, no revelation. Nevertheless, a peculiar focus and bond had been achieved or received. The forlorn downtrodden image in the window embedded itself within my being and thrives even today. A form of commitment had been made that night, although I know not to whom, with what, or how. There was no recognizable communication in the traditional sense of the word. There was merely the knowledge of the all-consuming attempt and perhaps a memorable *fragmentary-touching-upon*, struck within my being. I had failed in my attempt to reach my mother—but had I actually failed?

With the intervening interlude and with homage to hindsight, I believe the concentration—the unheard sound, which startled me alert—and the resultant shock peering into my own haggard reflection caused to reinforce, or more likely to solidify, to actually propel a destined path, the pathway that henceforth culminated in a miraculous decisive mystical event, a distant twenty-two years later.

Fortuitous Desire—The Author's Story

What made you begin to write poetry? Now, that is a tale worth telling—briefly! As near as I can recall, in my youth I began to search for, call it what you will, a superior power, superior being, God, perhaps a greater meaning. I silently prayed devotedly each night. With due concentration, on occasion I would hear what I perceived to be a faraway heavenly music akin to an orchestra all tuning up. This *connection* was difficult to achieve, yet not too difficult, as the music could indeed be heard when sincerely desired and focused upon. I would listen and simultaneously wonder at the source of the sound.

## Margaret Mary Stender

There is currently no recollection of when the music began or how it first approached or appeared. As near as I can determine at this juncture in life, the music lasted only perhaps six months to a year or two. A poem titled *Harken Low to Listen,* dated February 17, 1996, (See Appendix), forty-three to forty-seven years later, was written to commemorate the rapturous heavenly music. Yet the poem was instigated because the music played a prominent role in youth and was never dissuaded nor forgotten. The irony is that it was written only after the influence, and under the influence, of a recently acquired faculty that will shortly be expounded upon.

Years after the music appeared, while working in the Office of the City Treasure, Kalamazoo, Michigan, I expressly remember walking to the local bookstore to purchase a book to alleviate, or to satisfy, the insatiable spiritual yearning that continually badgered and plagued me. Once in the bookstore, while staring at the titles and pondering what and where to begin, a book suddenly dropped from a bookshelf. The shelf was located higher than the forward line of my vision. It dropped immediately in front and landed on the floor right at my feet. To my astonishment, Annalee Skarin's *Ye Are Gods* wondrously presented itself to me.

In February 1973, near the time of the bookshelf incident, I somehow became aware of Richard Maurice Bucke's book *Cosmic Consciousness,* of persons in possession of the Cosmic Sense. In the early 1900s, Bucke listed and elaborated upon the experiences of forty great persons of history, and pronounced and established many of these persons as having received the ultimate *gift, faculty;* the gift of what he termed Cosmic Consciousness (Endnote 1); namely, a consciousness of the cosmos, or a consciousness of the universe; of the life and order of the universe; the divine faculty; or Illumination, frequently known as Enlightenment.

Bucke explains that at the onset of illumination, persons may become aware of the visual appearance of a subjective light, or of flame. He further describes the illumination experience itself based upon his personal knowledge. More specifically, he elaborates upon the entire *process*, in large part using the words of numerous other persons who also possessed direct personal knowledge. He describes the prelude to the experience and its net result, the new faculty, in depth.

Bucke determined that after illumination, there exists—and thrives—a moral elevation and an intellectual illumination within each individual. Each person also possesses an overwhelming sense of immortality. He emphatically states that the faculty of Cosmic Consciousness may be identified by a combination of what he calls the Marks of Cosmic Sense.

In those early years, my heart, my mind, and I believe my soul, craved, and, thereafter, consumed the contents of *Cosmic Consciousness*. What more could one ask for? What more indeed...

The time of my young adulthood was precious as it is for everyone who is delightfully embroiled in raising a family; while still struggling to earn a suitable living; while undertaking the normal daily routine; namely, in managing the unique responsibilities of a busy to a harried adult life. All worldly duties took their toll and frequently, to my perception and chagrin, appeared to inhibit conscious spiritual growth. There never seemed to be enough time. And certainly, there was never sufficient time to read or to glean sorely sought-after spiritual insight in an attempt to settle the turmoil of a wandering soul. The interior being seemed to cry out for just compensation.

Thenceforth, in an endeavor to satisfy the inner life, the craving and tremendous aching-need to search for what I will call the Eternal, and with the lack of abiding time, I vowed to concentrate on, to read and to learn, whenever, wherever, adequate time prevailed. To the maximum extent feasible, I vowed to acquire and to concentrate solely on the writings of those illumined persons named in Bucke's *Cosmic Consciousness*.

With the assistance of the purchasing department director, Willard Kane, in 1974, I managed to order bound copies of the entire four volumes of *The Works of Jacob Behmen* (Endnote 2) from University Microfilm, located in Ann Arbor. At my suggestion, this company apparently secured the original books from the University.

Throughout the next several decades these four extensive volumes, I would like to say, were my constant companions, but that is not entirely true. They were at least intermittent, albeit sparse, companions. The concepts behind Behmen's writings were so completely beyond my comprehension in the beginning that, due to the need for deep concentration, they put me directly to sleep. Still, eventually, many of the general concepts settled in.

A vast number of years elapsed wherein I managed all of the duties of a responsible wife and mother and also tended to my spiritual life to the greatest extent feasible, or, perhaps, not to the greatest extent feasible. Still, I read. I learned. These were good years. These were also treacherous years. At some point during the ups and downs, I realized that *Leaves of Grass*, by Walt Whitman, one of Bucke's "designees," was completely beyond my grasp. Whitman's book was soon set aside and appeared to hold no future with me.

Nevertheless, in early 1991, with some form of interior instigation, I once again picked up *Leaves of Grass* and now realized that Whitman was endowed with significantly greater insight and depth than I had been able to apprehend or appreciate in my younger years. This time when I read his poetry, I automatically recognized correlations with a few of the points established in the writings of Jacob Behmen, as well as with the writings about or by other illumined persons.

This is where the story and question, "What made you begin to write poetry?" and ultimately the book, *A Tiny but Radiant Light*, truly begins. This is where the *Prelude* to the true mystical revelation staunchly stands.

## CHAPTER II
## Endnotes

Endnote 1
   Bucke, Richard Maurice, M.D., *Cosmic Consciousness,* New York, E. P. Dutton and Company, Inc., Publisher, Fourteenth Edition. 1948, p 3.

Endnote 2
   *The Works of Jacob Behmen*, the Teutonic Theosopher, with Figures, illustrating his Principles, left by the Reverend William Law, M. R. London, Printed for M. Richardson, in Pater-noster Row, MDCCLXIV

COMMENT:
   *A Tiny but Radiant Light* contains an undue number of endnotes; yet to avoid breaking the continuity of the primary narrative, it seems prudent to incorporate pertinent analogous information as an endnote. This is particularly true in the case of John Middleton Murry.

Margaret Mary Stender

## CHAPTER III

## EVENING AND MOMENT—Espousal of Above and Below

Recognition of Something, Soon to Occur

I poured over and soon devoured *Leaves of Grass*. Unexpectedly, within a few months I began to perceive a unique rhythm, a growing awareness that while reading Whitman's work, a deep sense of peace would engender my mood, and an intriguing pleasant-pulsation, a mild rhythmic or quavering feeling, would accompany the reading and waylay, would soothe, my body: This was the most exceptionally inviting feeling.

Increasingly, after prolonged periods of reading, an instilled thoughtful mood, accompanied by a mild trembling would linger for hours after the reading ended. I delighted in the poetry, and especially in its prolonged beneficial mental and physical effects. Every spare hour was devotedly shared with Whitman. (Endnotes 1, 2)

After reading for a solid five months, and by virtue of the induced rhythm, by late July, Wednesday, July 24, twenty plus years after my mother's death (though, no longer strenuously influenced by my mother's death), in some unknown intuitive manner, I knew, seriously I knew, to vow not to go to sleep that night until I "found" God; Jacob wrestled with the Lord—I will not let you go except Thou bless me—and numerous persons, of whom I was aware through Bucke's writing, had been illumined. The potential was apparent to my mind and justified my intent.

I was aware of the possibility of illumination; of a few of its modes of flaming spontaneously into existence; of the momentary surprise or quandary of mind of the recipient during the onset; of the immanent knowledge; and of the inevitable new faculties with their multiple aspects.

Never in my wildest dreams, however, would I have ever believed that a similar extraordinary experience could actually occur with me. Yet, on that particular evening I was determined to "wrestle with the Lord" by staying awake throughout the night and reading to perpetuate the increasingly pronounced mild pulsing feeling, a rhythm which now wholly engendered itself and engulfed me while reading *Leaves of Grass*.

Somehow, I knew that this profound rhythm would bring about some form of experience. I planned to read unto the brink of wakefulness or sleepiness, until s*omething* happened. To my mind, the struggle to stay awake was akin to Jacob's wrestling with the Angel of the Lord. I would stay awake all night if need be.

I could feel there was the potential for an inspirational experience or a spiritual awakening, albeit nothing as grand as pure enlightenment, just *something*, merely something! The intuitive knowledge was alert and valid. Intuition enhanced or propounded by Whitman's rhythm was superfluous and pronounced. The multifarious feeling was immediate and alluring.

I was compelled. I knew, and, again, *I knew that I knew*, that an experience could happen, not would happen, but could happen. I was inwardly driven by measures considerably beyond my active earthly comprehension. I cannot expound upon this point enough. In a situation such as this, pure ordinary head knowledge does not enter in. Though, even in my naiveté, I was determined.

> *Reader, please excuse this temporary interruption in relating the story of the mystical evening and moment— the "moment" constitutes the Moment of the Enkindling—and for shifting so abruptly to a coexistent topic. However, as a delayed result of this selfsame evening, a poem was written titled "Megan's Story."*

## Margaret Mary Stender

*This inspired and lengthy poem, written in December 1994, constitutes a concise general overview of certain preceding elements of this exemplary evening; of the mystical moment; of ensuing moments; and of the immediate and forth-birthing faculties.*

*Though written considerably after-the-fact, this true poetic account was penned while still under the all-encompassing influence of the evening, and specifically of the precise moment of interaction, the conjunction—the enkindling—and also under the more recent overarching influence of the poetry.*

*During the writing, an extraordinary level of inspiration, emotion, and intuitive knowledge was in vital attendance. Therefore, it is prudent to periodically interpose verses from "Megan's Story" and other applicable poems throughout this narrative. (Yet, for continuity, merely, reading the narrative is initially superior.)*

*The inspired rhythmic nature of the poetry differs dramatically from this informative narrative. Note the change in tone, Note the simplicity.*

*The poetry was created while the gifts, and the related feeling of physical well-being, were actively "living" in all of their vitality in the mind and body.*

*The dates of the individual poems provide a degree of chronology.*

### Selection from *Megan's Story*

*She read about all the enlightened, Jacob Behmen.*
*And later, "Hit upon" Walt Whitman. So profound were these men*
*That she never left and will never leave them.*

*With her knowledge, earthly though it was, and is fragmented.*
*And though the knowledge was considered by a mediocre mind,*

*Yet she recognized the similarities within them,*
*The direction they were to provide, along with knowledge*

## A Tiny But Radiant Light

*Of the others, of those blessed enlightened,*
*Dearly beloved revered of men.*

*Megan then in faith, and in consideration,*
*Of Jacob wrestling with the Lord,*
*Knew that she could follow his direction, Megan more than knew*
*She knew for she could feel the rhythm of Walt's poetry,*
*Working, strangely over time within her chest and arms,*

*And within her head...And how she knew, I do not know.*

*One night she said to herself and to God,*
*"Tonight I wrestle with the Lord,*
*And I will not sleep until you bless me."*
*Walt Whitman will I read, the rhythm to be felt,*
*Until dawn or until you bless me.*

I went to bed early; read to the point of sleepiness; continued reading long into the night; dozed off, aroused myself immediately; read, dozed, read, dozed, read, dozed, and read and read. At a certain point, I fell asleep all together. Shortly thereafter, I startled awake with the sharp memory of the compelling words of a verse that had thrust itself into my head. The emergence was sufficiently intense that I was constrained to get up to write the words to assure a remembrance.

To my immense surprise, when I arose from the bed, my equilibrium was nonexistent. I stumbled into the bed, into the wall, and into the doorway. *Something,* other than the receipt of the few words had occurred, had genuinely usurped my equilibrium. I knew not what. Neither did I understand. And, neither was I aware that the words constituted a foreshadow of the events to come.

A pencil and paper were located and the words recorded. Weary and barely half-awake, I believed the prolonged effort of reading was *sufficient* and that what had just occurred constituted the extent of the "S*omething* soon to occur." The verse and loss of equilibrium constituted the "unknown" which I had anticipated, and it had been achieved. Not realizing, not possessing a clue or having an inclination as to what astonishment was yet to come, I said to myself, "I think it is all right now to go to sleep."

The words of the verse which were thrust into my being were structured as in a poem-like semblance, and the entirety was titled, *Love the World Doth "Own."*

Selection from *Megan's Story*

*So Megan read late into the night, then slightly unknowingly dozed,*
*Then roused herself her promise to keep to wrestle with the Lord,*
*And read again, then dozed again, and arose again, and dozed again,*
*And aroused again and read the book—Walt Whitman's book.*

*In faith she maintained her vigilance, yet sleep overcame her,*
*With that sleep this night a dream awoke her,*
*Instantly giving her a poem, she arose to the occasion,*
*And said, "It is so beautiful. I must arise to write it down."*

*The pencil in the other room, "I must find to record." She arose*
*From the bed, much to her amazement she could not walk a-right,*
*She stumbled into the bed then the wall and opposite wall,*
*Her equilibrium was no more, she was completely out of balance,*
*And barely made it to the pencil to record the lovely poem,*
*The gift that was given that night to write it down.*

    Love the World Doth Own

    *Come forth in me,*
    *Shine through me.*
    *Guide me, thrill me,*
    *Fill me with great love,*
    *For all the love,*
    *The world doth own,*
    *Belongs to Thee.*
    *7/24/1991*

*As she stumbled back to bed,*
*Within herself I heard her say,*

# A Tiny But Radiant Light

*"I think it is all right now to go to sleep,"*
*The easy way out again, but she did.*

## Thunderous Sound: The Enkindling—The Crowning

Within a few moments, pleased with myself and expecting nothing more, while soundly sleeping, the mind, alerted, sprung open to a secondary or alternate level of consciousness. A consciousness arose, which is completely focused within its own selfhood, self-knowledge or self-awareness, without reference or recourse to the senses or any material thing normally manifest to the exterior senses; having access only to the knowledge pertinent to the episode at hand and to no other; specifically entirely focused, actually absorbed in, or being one with the immediate—as it relates to thought about or concerning the immediate.

(This description is exceedingly difficult as, once again, I know of no word to effectively describe or to relay the concept of this honed and absorbent level of consciousness. Or, possibly, A.P. Sinnett stated it more precisely, though, in a slightly differing context: "—this is the important point to realize—cease for the time to be conscious of the physical realm. It does not exist for them..." [Endnote 3])

I had been abruptly awakened to an intensity of sound, the loud thunderous raging of swiftly rushing winds breaking-forth through the darkness, surging toward me, striking and spontaneously infusing me with its unique sympathetic rhythm: (With no perceived interval of elapsed time between the awakening with the breaking through the darkness with the recognition of the raging winds, and when the winds arrived and struck, delivered) a sudden enkindling, an immense crowning, a recognized intimate-pulsation in the middle of the head toward the top, thence flaring or flashing upward slightly over the head, then downward toward the shoulders. Then slowly, perceptively, the pronounced pulsing-sensation spread slowly out through the arms into the hands then into the fingers. Only then, did it perceptively begin to edge down the chest. My consciousness accompanied the movement of the enkindling of the physical—the uniting—in stunned awe.

In my comprehension, with the analytical "part of" mind, I, then, clearly recall thinking, "When *It* reaches the area of my heart, it will burst into flame." (Although, that was *the* thought, a better description or explanation is that the *pulsation* would ignite into flame, visibly perceptible internally.) The purely overt and self-seeking self-serving intrusive modicum of knowledge, gleaned from earnest reading in the past, impressed itself in the form of one prominent *exterior* extraneous, annihilating, soul-provoking, thought; a thought belonging to the normal consciousness, the self-consciousness.

The movement, the traveling of the striking physical manifestation, all striking pulsation, the mystical rapture, the enkindling with its traveling ecstasy, stopped instantly. It just disappeared! It was gone with no relenting, no retrieving back.

Simultaneously, with the overt annihilating thought, the secondary level of consciousness dissolved leaving merely wonder at its presentation and rendering, and near-pure disgust at its departure. (Due solely to this experience, I realize that one does not "think" in the normal manner when enveloped within an alternative consciousness, but one simply lives and notices and relates to the "circumstance" directly-*at-hand* internally. No perception of the outward senses is ever considered. An individual recognizes the difference in consciousness only at the point of departure from the alternative consciousness.)

I wept silent light tears, recognizing—a comprehension more grand than mere knowledge, a *Knowing*—that this priory gift was, is, of divine origin. Concurrently, I knew that if this majestic experience had only occurred once in fifty-two years that it was unlikely to occur again. I wept in praise, and in glory and thankfulness, and in impassioned veneration. I also wept in sadness, in prolific indefinable regret, in the certain knowledge that this unifying moment may never reoccur.

I rested blessed, rapt in the profound lingering effects of the rhythm; of the newly formally instilled mild lingering pulsation of a blessed calm; of an overflowing love; of an inborn sacred knowledge; of this majesty in ecstasy. The *Moment* of revelation had dawned an inexpressible boundless Love: a love burgeoning outward.

A selection from *Megan's Story* appears in the Appendix.

### Knowledge Known—Entwined with Thunderous Sound—The Endkindling

"Knowledge Known" harks back to and should be tightly entwined with "Thunderous Sound." Nonetheless, due to their unique characteristics and for the sake of clarity, herein they are considered independently and distinguished separately. (Endnotes 4, 5)

By birthright, Knowledge Known commands full heir-ship with Thunderous Sound, though more especially, more profoundly, it is shared with the Enkindling. Knowledge Known flares equally with the breaking through the darkness (an awakened consciousness), and is also the astute awareness, the intuitive knowing, brought about by and of the life-birthing Enkindling, with its interaction (the authoritative knowledge, the knowledge embedded, in-birthed, Known! [Endnote 6]).

Thunderous Sound, the pulsing winds, deliver the enkindling, which Enkindling, Itself, ignites, is the ignition (the espousal of above and below—a conjunction of the infinite and the finite), and the consequent intimate-rapture flares, and is borne aloft (*bursts* within the head and flashes aloft [Endnotes 7, 8]) coexistent with, meaning generated by, the vibratory rhythmic *waves* of the Thunderous Sound—the winds.

The enkindling precedes and conveys the resultant possession of the faculty—illumination, enlightenment—which faculty is acquired immediately, birthed as the direct consequence of the espousing of the especial enkindling. The enkindling also implants that faculty which awakens the individual to the knowledge of an everlasting life, of immortality—the cardinal Knowledge Known!

## Margaret Mary Stender

(Endowed gifts are delineated in the succeeding section, *New Life Living Within—The Life Speaks Out in You*.) Lessor gifts, or attributes, may be inbred or recognized over a period of time.

Knowledge Known and Thunderous Sound are greater than twins. They are conjoined mates. The two cannot be subdivided. As previously stated, they are birthed together, just prior to (but, with no perceptible lapse in "time") the delivery—the strike—of the enkindling.

### Poetry in Affirmation of the Knowledge Known

### When Knowledge Knows Itself to Be

*There is a knowledge now so firmly etched withon the brain,*
    *that permeates the mind, that no amount of earthly force,*

*No rationalization, no logic, no other weary, dreary, mental work*
    *or fatigue, can wear away, or tear away, peel or separate*
    *the knowledge which is known.*

*The knowledge which is known, has merged as a part,*
    *now known, indwells itself, forming one united whole.*
*And as a basic element, the one missing withon the periodic chart,*
    *can not be divided, not subdivided,*

*Exists as one, the knowledge thus and us. As one*
    *becomes, has become a part, the living conscious*
*Knows itself to be the faithfulness—faith substantial.*
    *It is and knows and tells us so, so willingly and gently.*

*As grows the dew withon the herbage,*
    *as grows the dawn withon the day,*
*As comes and is the substantiality of sunlit noon,*
    *grows the knowledge known.*

*Withof itself it knows, knows and tells us so,*
    *—the life of immortality.*
        *8/26/1997 The Forever Entwined (TFE)*

## A Tiny But Radiant Light

### The Overflowing, the Gush and Wane
### —Its Knowingness Upon Thy Soul

*There are no words of—my personal—wisdom here*
    *and ever have there never been,*
*Though thankfulness and gratefulness,*
    *and joy and everlasting mirth abounding,*
*The overflowing, the gush and wane, the thought,*
    *articulated, in whatever vein,*
*Poured forth itself and abounded,*
    *alight with love, alive with hope and praise.*

*(Or, O let my correction be—no Hope,*
    *abounds with thoughts of me, for Hope*
    *has been surmounted,*
*Only Faith, substantiated unrelenting anticipation,*
    *for the One, the One of all—and of all opportunity,*
*In here, here upon this Earth,*
    *and for and in all eternity.)*

*And if a word or two, inspires or encourages you,*
    *or if the Spirit alights withon within,*
*Then know and see and be, the love abounding,*
    *the joy instilled, the gracious glowing,*
*The solemn and silent calm, the peace a-floating.*
    *And, eventually, thou shall see the love abounding*
*Rightfully with thee, shall take thee hand a-hold, firm hand*
    *a-hold, its knowingness, upon thy soul,*
*And thee shall rhyme, or speak, or sing, or pray, or sit*
    *and joy, and thee the peacemaker, thee shall be.*
    *10/26/1998 TFE*

Margaret Mary Stender

# CHAPTER III
## Endnotes

Endnote 1

It is important to mention at the onset that the descriptive words, trembling, quivering, pulsing, quavering, fluttering, tremulous, etc., used throughout this work, are not precisely correct. No single word comes to mind that would be considered ultimately adequate or all-encompassing. Nevertheless, in differing degrees and under differing circumstances, each of these words are near. It is as the wind with instigation to blow gentle and mild, or eager and joyful.

Endnote 2

As Yogi Raushan Nath would confide, "The vibrations produced by the mantra recitation excite similar vibrations in the listeners. (It is a known phenomenon that a singer can make a musical instrument vibrate in consonance, provided he sings at the same frequency at which the said instrument is set.)." *THE UNSEEN HAND*, a handbook of yoga way of life for self-realization, YOGI RAUSHAN NATH, Foreword by DR. KARAN SINGH, RAJIV PUBLICATIONS, NEW DELHI, June 1971. Distributors: Trimuri Publications, W-152, Greater Kailash-I, New Delhi-48. PRINTED IN INDIA BY: NEW INDIAN PRESS, K-BLOCK, CONNAUGHT CIRCUS, NEW DELHI-1. *OM ! THE PRANAVA, MANTRA: ITS SPIRITUAL STAMNIA*, p 243.

Endnote 3

*Collected Fruits of Occult Teaching,* London, T. FISHER UNVIN, LTD. Adelphi Terrace, p 35.

Endnote 4

A distinctive intuitive knowledge exists, the knowledge of the unity and the harmony of the cosmos, as described and propounded by Bucke, and which is in-birthed, or delivered, to individuals attaining to illumination. This is also the Knowledge Known which is derived by virtue of the moment of the enkindling: nonetheless, Knowledge

# A Tiny But Radiant Light

Known may be engifted to a marginal degree or range from nominal to phenomenal, comparatively speaking.

Endnote 5

Another example of the definition of Knowledge is to be found at: Internet, Sacred-Texts. com. Basil Valentine, 1700s, *Trimphal Chariot of Antimony*: "Operation of the Hands requires a diligent application of it self, But the praise of Science consists in experience, but the difference of these *Anatomy* distinquisheth, Operations shew how all things may be brought to light, and exposed to sight visibly: but knowledge shews the practice; and that, whence the true Practitioner is, and is no other then confirmation: because the operation of the hands manifest something that is good and draws the latent and hidden nature outwards, and brings it to light for good."

Endnote 6

Realization—Max Freedman Long, in *The Secret Science Behind Miracles,* DeVorss & Co., *Publishers,* 4900 Eagle Rock Blvd., Los Angeles, Calif., Copyright 1948. 1954 Second Edition, p 118.

The definition Long uses to define a process of knowing seems to precisely describe what I have continually comprehended and represented in this work as pure "Knowing." Long says, of what he has termed the superconscious, "The superconscious uses, according to my conclusions, a form of thinking higher than either memory or reason, although it seems capable of remembering and reasoning. The only word in English to describe this thinking process is 'realization'—a process of knowing things without going through the labor of remembering and applying logic to what is remembered and what is being observed."

Endnote 7

Born and also borne with the conjunction, the enkindling and resultant flash, is the immediate perception and recognition, a distinct knowledge, of an adjoining, which furthers itself into the future.

Endnote 8

"Bursts" is an inadequate word. Perhaps, "blossoms" is more appropriate, yet it bursts, as it is spontaneous, unexpected and sudden.

## CHAPTER IV

## NEW LIFE LIVING WITHIN—The Life Speaks Out In You

Words cannot describe nor awe express "what" occurred during those wondrous moments of the divine mystical enkindling, nor, can one faithfully describe the magnitude of the effects of the newly acquired faculty; though, this endeavor is dedicated to trying.

To my personal perception, the initial gifts include a suffused sacred Calm, a laudable Presence; a riotous bounteous Joy; a Youth within; and an abounding prolific Eternal Love, a love beyond earthly comprehension and description; Love unites with the *individual*; ameliorates the individual. It appears to shine forth from within and propels the *two*, now one, forth-ward in continuity, in generosity.

Moreover, pursuant to this perception, Eternal Love exists for no one individual, nor any specific endeavor, but for its life, its purpose, its giving, its yielding, its granting, its generosity—to the entirety, underneath and throughout. To the common consciousness it loves, it glows without apparent reason, for its own inevitable infinite purpose.

### Calm—The Silence Under the Sound

To reiterate and expound upon that which is briefly set forth in *First Words*, the first week after the evening of the enkindling, there was a deep immersion in the remotest sea of calm. Anger and impatience virtually dissolve; they become nonexistent; there is no hatred, there is no ire.

# A Tiny But Radiant Light

The Calm portends to a "distancing." The distancing, an indifference, a limited detachment, is an offshoot or an effect of the Calm; a distancing from harsh or adverse emotion, or from a rise to heightened emotion, when, in truth, prior to the enkindling, a true or a perceived negative outward activity, circumstance, or the spoken word, would have caused a reaction.

The outward worldly effects are not absorbed, or borne as a weight or a burden—nor as a conscience—as most problems or troubles are borne, as we recognize the *role* of conscience today. Concurrently, material possessions become less important to totally unimportant.

In the writings and poetry, the Calm is occasionally referred to as a lull due to its ability to mediate or halt the influence of the exterior or natural world, to instill a nonchalance of all natural activity; it mellows. To my belief, the Calm equates in stature to the first cousin of the "peace that passeth all understanding." One can not sufficiently applaud this calmness, this presence: it is a peaceful harmonious bliss, as a still glassy lake with no ripple and no rancor.

This majestic mystical event occurred on a Wednesday night extending into early Thursday morning. Thursday, there was no choice. I had to go to work. For one solid week, I lived in a sea of perpetual calm. I walked through the daily necessities as if by rote, or just sat at my desk or at home, accomplishing nothing and non-caring. I was benumbed. My work soon fell way behind. Realizing there was no choice but to work, little by little I brought myself back into the world of activity, to accomplishing on the material plane only what absolutely had to be done.

Though, for one extraordinary week there was an ultimate peace and a perpetual calm that surpass expression and astound understanding. It knows no rush. It knows no necessity. It knows no boundary. It abided with me as a light dew is apparent. It knew that whatever *I did* ultimately did not matter, anyway. It knew of eternity. It knew no death. It knew, and consisted of peace, of love, of affection, of understanding. It knew of a knowledge generally unsought and definitely generally unknown. It knew, and now I knew.

Margaret Mary Stender

Poetry in Desire of the Sea of Perpetual Calm
Prevalent within the Soul

### In Simplicity and Stillness Sat

*As Whistler's mother sat, in calm and peace of mind,*
   *looking only withon the inside in,*
*So sat the child-servant of God, one time,*
   *looking only, seeing only withon the within.*

*The what was within, was the permeation—a Stillness*
   *—sounding, clambering, shrieking, near inaudibly,*
*Benumbingly. Perceived with every pore discerned by every cell,*
   *known by every excellence and attribute and faculty,*
*Comprehended by virtue and sanctity and patience,*
   *established by truth and righteousness.*

*As Whistler's mother sat, in calm and peace of mind,*
   *looking only withon the inside in,*
*So sat the child-servant of God, one time,*
   *looking only, feeling only withon the within.*
       *2/10/1998 TFE*

*This Day Awakening Tempering* and *Lull—The Crown of Pearl* appear in the Appendix.

### Laudable Presence—The Bounty of Calm

*A distinct feeling* well out-of-the-ordinary that could only be described as a living Presence, lived actively with me in a greater or less degree, with various accompanying gifts, for many years. The Presence principally stayed, lived and guided me in its quiescent fashion for only three plus months. Then—the horrendous blow—the City, my employer, received a massive task from the Department of Housing and Urban Development, the Area Office in Detroit. Instinctively, I knew that to accomplish it, or to even address it, I must effectively set this "gift," this feeling, this awareness, this togetherness, this composed peacefulness, this presence, this calm, aside in order to accomplish the task.

After long consideration, then short delay, I tackled the duty of necessity with the vigor and ingenuity needed, and immediately lost the majority of the balance of the peace and calm with its slight pulsation, and the gift of the intense presence. A relatively bare skeleton or remnant remained compared to before.

(There was the initial colossal loss of the perpetual calm after one week. Then there was a second reduction, the presence with the ever-so-slight weight, its calm, after three plus months, which dealt a rigorous blow. Thereafter, the differing levels or degrees of the various combinations of the gifts abided as in hills and valleys.)

### Selection from *Megan's Story*

*The blessedness had descended upon her,*
*And for within one week, she could only sit and consider.*
*She would get up and go to work, and sit and ponder*
    *in wonderment,*
*And watch the work stack itself in unconcern and non-caring.*

*Megan knew that no matter what she did or did not do,*
*It did not matter. Ultimately it did not matter.*
*She could work, or non-work all the same,*
*And it really would not matter: all are "saved" ultimately.*
*And she knew that she knew and she knew that too.*

*One week she sat in wonderment, in nonchalance,*
*In an abatement of all care, concern,*
*She was living in a lull of contentment, sitting just feeling*
*The presence that had descended upon her*
*Was still living and feeling within her.*

*Then she had to go to work, the presence understood,*
*And assisted from that point forth always assisted in its slow,*
*And unintrusive way and it stayed three months plus,*
*A living, jointly, joyfully, mutually within her.*

## Margaret Mary Stender

*Megan nurtured this presence in love and thoughtfulness,*
*In her new now milder way, until a heavy task was upon her,*
*To accomplish and she shoved the beloved presence aside,*
*To permit her access to her full earthly capability,*
*Her task to undertake, for with the presence,*
*The difficult arduous task she could not do.*

*Now Megan well-nigh lost her gift*
*Through her naivety and her foolishness,*
*Ever to regret and never to now to recover.*

As just previously stated, though this is critical and bears elaboration and celebration, for the first week, I existed in a lull; a perpetual calm. Then for three plus months the presence lived actively with me; I apprehended its restfulness, its affection. It made itself prominent. After three plus months and for many years, it still lived on in varying degrees and with varying effects—as a wave which ebbed and flowed, but ever lower. Its presence and physical effect never completely left, nor left my mind. We basked together in its light, the light of peace and love, for a multitude of years.

### Poetry in Celebration of the Presence Within

### The Lull

*It is like a white misty dew and it stands still and lives in you,*
*It tranquilizes, soothes and lulls, in its unknowing doing,*
*And brings you, the this of you, into its tranquility too,*
*It harbors no ill effects, it loves and lulls,*

*It is quiet and solemn, resting upon,*
*Within, your being as presence,*
*It knows no death, no mortality, it neutralizes,*
*Instills a knowing, not knowledge, but knowing*
*of the One within the all.*
*1/21/1996 (TGS)*

# A Tiny But Radiant Light

## Love Eternal—O My Virgin Sophia, O My Noble Love

During the succeeding several-year period, varying gifts and pleasantries continually abided within. Especially apparent was a thriving abounding love; a growing, glowing radiant love which generated an ecstatic joy and which was accompanied by an impassioned unfathomable faith; a knowing. (Endnote 1)

The every day's long-term affect of the Love—when at its ultra-height—is similar to the perception received during the enkindling, the conflagration, when the flash flared upward above the head (Endnotes 2). The Love and I were distinctly one. That momentous evening, the feeling, the awareness, of the physical being literally extended beyond the boundary of the body, namely it extended above the head, enlarging the being momentarily with its selfsame assurance and perception.

Thereafter, on certain rare occasions, the Love beamed without, outside, the physical body, in the vicinity of the level of the chest, making one feel as if they were literally larger than one's self—though, in this instance, there is no awareness within the extension.

O how can I express the feeling when love expands outside the body for a distance, as a welling expands? Normally love, not at its height, though, radiating, maintains itself within the constructs of the natural physical body, but no larger than the physical body. The Virgin Sophia streams and beams and knows no boundary.

Unlike, the Calm, which was born—streamed into the world majestic—with the enkindling, then faded at every trial, the Love, born delicate and subtle, began with veneration and grew to enormous bounds.

## Margaret Mary Stender

## Poetry in Light of the Love

### Selection from *To Hold One's Mind Aloft*

*"A great love was born within our ranks*
    *and sometimes flickers and sometimes flames,*
*And that Love is not ours, but is in and throughout all time*
    *throughout all eternity—and it glitters and it shines.*
*Love 'flows' within and without throughout—it moves*
    *and stands stock-still-and it yields and it gives."*
    *5/29/1998 TGS*

### Ignited, the Light Lives

*Ignited, the light, the love, speaks*
    *forth into the outer world,*
*Unknown, unperceived, unseen*
    *—sometimes seen and denied,*
*Though, it lives in, and brings the*
    *Heavenly in and to the outer world.*
    *10/27/1995 TGS*

### Love thus Tendering Encircles

*O Prophet heavenly, today, this day, again today,*
    *my heart is swelling welling out,*
*The feelings that are born inside are borne*
    *and beam and blossom all about.*

*This fondness thus is born within my breast*
    *transmits its ray a streaming—gleaming*
*A fountain up, a cascade down, sprays, arrays,*
    *adorns the love around in equal measure.*

*So fine, so fair, so mild as air, so pure*
    *as light in darkness, unfound, is there,*
*So to the love thus tendering encircles, melodious,*
    *harmonious, harmonizing, synthesizing,*

## A Tiny But Radiant Light

*Synchronizing all interactions of those*
*so attuned to cull its wondrous virtue.*
*11/14/1995 TGS*

*As the Love Doth Live, O Gentle Ennoble Man, and O Gentle Ennoble Man—Expounded* appears in the Appendix.

### Riotous Bounteous Joy—Over Joyousness Expounding

When in the light of love, the human heart is alight with joy; joy, boundless superfluous joy! Joy seems to reach out to incorporate whatever and whomever is within its *sight*—is within *your* sight. It elevates one to unheard of heights. One feels as if they are glowing with joy! If a person could only, would only, even temporarily, drop their doubt and despair and believe, truly believe in the Joy, it will strengthen its activity and brighten, lighten, and enlighten, the proverbial *load*. Laughter, joyous rebellious sanctifying laughter, in its broad song, will be silently sung and will be silently heard.

Joy can be joyous regardless of the worldly surroundings. If one *listens* closely, one can feel the Joy emanating from their being. It is similar to the music of childhood inherent in one's being. Joy speaks no evil. Joy is unselfish and attributes to another. Joy hearkens to listen, to reach out, and to help. The counsel from the mouth of Joy is profound, second only to its kin, the voice of Love.

### Poetry in Appreciation of the Illustrious Joy

#### The Warble

*The Warble,*
*From the Soul,*
*Is Joy.*
        10/27/1994 Behold the Daybreak (BTD)

# Margaret Mary Stender

## O Joy, Thou Livest as a Flame

*O Joy, thou livest as a flame embrightening,*
*Thou dwellest in the heart and sproutest as a flower,*
*The joyfulness a color and savor and fragrance arising.*

*Woe be to the longing listlessness (Endnote 6),*
  *with Joy and hope arising,*
*Woe be to the ardent longing, with joyfulness a beaming*
  *streaming.*

*The Joy as radiation, sweet heat and warmth, overcomes,*
  *supersedes, super-passes, the dreariness of*
    *anguishing longing linger, and maintains*
      *it semi-withunder control.*
*Then O, it bursts, the longing bursts, erupts, and surges,*
  *a volcano typifying, weeps, and flowing lava seeps,*
    *and surging obliterates all in view, then halts,*

*And rays of warmth and glowing embers flowing light,*
  *so radiate and generate and flourish and nourish,*
    *inhabit, and quell,*
      *so mildly quell the earthly rush*
        *and mediate unholy ire.*

*O so, O Joy, thou art a King, at least a Prince,*
  *for the Princedom that thee holds*
    *second only to the Love and Light*
      *and the peaceful exalted Calm.*
        *2/9/1998 TFE*

The *longing-listlessness* referenced in the above poem, is that state which is endured as it accompanies the detrimental decline, as it longs for the gift that is declining or is nearly lost. The detrimental decline is addressed later in this narrative.

# A Tiny But Radiant Light

## Sounding Forth the Joy

*Lo those many years,*
    *the glorious, mysterious, generous,*
*The seven years culminating in today,*
    *the date, the anniversary,*
*The ups and downs and side-wise, back,*
    *though, O, the ups and downs*
*Of earthly consolation and tribulation,*
    *so minuscule, so remote,*
*The knowledge and the gifts having flamed*
    *into the advantage of the time,*
*Highlight, mellow, delicate, subtle,*
    *melodize and harmonize, synchronize,*
*All earthly woes and earthly walks,*
    *and reign supreme, the Love,*
*And as a trumpet plays sounding,*
    *Breathing-forth, the joy.*
        *7/24/1998 TFE*

## Poetry by Edward Carpenter, Speaks of the Joy

Edward Carpenter, a nineteenth century poet, speaks eloquently of the Joy. One can virtually feel the ardor radiating from his words and entering their being. Here we deviate temporarily from the primary narrative—the purpose of *A Tiny but Radiant Light* (Endnote 3)—and turn to *Towards Democracy* for further illustration of the passionate exhilaration—of the Joy—bred forth from the Love: a momentary sampling of joy:

    The word travels on.
    Out of the mists of time, out of innumerable births, of endless journeys, transfigurements, lives, deaths, sorrows, emerging, my voice sounds to myself, to you, nearer than all thought: tentatively trying the first notes, wonderingly at its beauty, of the Song-strange word!—of Joy.
    To spread abroad over the earth, to be realised in time: Freedom to be realised in time, for which the whole of History

has been a struggle and a preparation:
The dream of the soul's slow disentanglement. (Endnote 4)

To Savagery and the wild woods, with unfettered step; to rocks and hanging branches; to the dens of the animals, to wind and sun, blowing shining through, and I through them, to evade and arise;
With joy over the world, Democracy, born again, into heaven, over the mountain-peaks and the seas in the unfathomable air, screaming, with shouts of joy, whirling the nations with her breath. Into heaven arising and passing, I arise and pass—dreaming the dream of the soul's slow disentanglement. (Endnote 5)

Happiness does not proceed by chance, nor is got by supplication, but is inevitable wherever the Master is.
Doubt parts aside. I hear grown and bearded men shouting in the woods for joy, shouting singing with the birds; I hear the immense chorus over all the world, of the Return to Joy.

Come, my friend, in the still autumn morning, while the sun is yet low upon the hills, among the dead leaves come walk with me.
Those and the like of those that have been my companions are with you also, and shall be to all time. I give you but a hint and a word of commendation. I open a door outwards. (Endnote 6)

O joy returning morn noon and night! day-long as in a dream walking over earth enchanted, waking deep midnight out of sleep in the ocean of joy! [Lo! The beautiful surface, the rippling of waves, the moon shining down.]
Deep deep draughts of all that life can give, drawn in to feed the flame—
Joy, joy and thanks for ever.
[O burning behind all worlds, immortal Essences, Flames of the ever-consuming universe, never-consumed—to laugh and laugh with you, and of our laughter
Shake forth creation!]. (Endnote 7)

# A Tiny But Radiant Light

## Youth Within—The Radiant Boy

Let us return to the gilded thread: the Youth Within reached overflowing, and was first spoken of in the poetry in March 1996, nearly five years after the evening and moment of the enkindling. Youth, issued by the Joy, constitutes a grand vibrant aspect. However, a curious idiosyncrasy accompanies the Youth; a mischievousness. When Youth radiates in joyousness—from joyousness—Youth appears to wish to exert and to proclaim *its* influence.

Ironically it did. Youth displayed *himself* in one peculiar respect and that was by winning drawings. These drawings were, for instance, small in nature such as the drawings entered as a part of a group: a garden club; a motor home travel group; or any form of gathering in which I was an integral part and participated along with every other member.

At a certain juncture, what Bucke would call the Self-Consciousness, or the self-conscious mind, what I would call my solely personal earthly self, the purely human aspect, became so embarrassed by the frequent winnings, and the erroneousness of winning, that it became sufficiently emotionally fraught to take it upon *itself* to inwardly *talk to*, to caution, and to mildly chastise the joyous youth within. (Perhaps, though I cannot prove it, perhaps, the youth is something of a prankster.)

Thereupon, I wrote a long-drawn out poem, *O Wondrous Child*, speaking to the youth of the necessity to "not win," nor to take advantage. Whereupon, the winning abruptly stopped. Nearly immediately thereafter, I was in serious trouble. Adamantly, the youth remained apparent beneath the conflict, joyous *by my side*, oblivious to the what-should-be apparent turmoil. This joyousness in what should be serious distress so flabbergasted the conscious mind that another poem was written titled, *Yet You Stayed, O Loyalty*.

The notion that the purely human aspect appeared to have more common sense than the cosmic influence—namely, the youthful influence—or especially to have the right to mildly chastise what I came to discern as the dependable youth within, appears to be presumptuous, outlandish and irresponsible.

Then, and especially now, the conscious mind realizes that there must have been a deeper, broader ground, an underlying role, a clearer understanding and *intention* welling behind and beyond the mere winning of small inconsequential drawings, the rationale of which was *known* only to the well-meaning Youth. This natural mind was not privy to the knowledge, was unable to comprehend the winnings, and believes the insight may never come to light.

Having related the lesson of the *drawings* and after nine years since the *Youth* poems were written, I should report that recently there was another incident at a class reunion. In the elevated exuberance and joy of the evening, I knew—and by saying "I knew," I knew—that I would win one of the drawings, sure enough a new embroidered shirt!

During the following few minutes a classmate who had traveled to Michigan from Texas, who was sitting next to me, won a flower arrangement. He turned around and gave it to me. Ultimately, naturally, the flower arrangement went home with another person. In total, there were about five prizes awarded. The youth may still occasionally play his pranks if for no other reason than to assure me that *he* is still around and bodes well. I love the joyous vibrant fellow, that wholesome energy.

Let us step aside another moment and relate Bucke's comment in *Cosmic Consciousness.*(Endnote 8) Bucke quoted Lamartine as saying about Honorè de Balzac: "A childlike merriment was in his aspect; here was a soul at play; he had dropped his pen to be happy among friends, and it was impossible not to be joyous where he was." (Endnote 9) The *childlike merriment* a description by Lamartine pertaining solely to Balzac, a distinctive man nearly unapproachable in his literary height, yet possessed a childlike merriment. This perfectly describes the youth within.

The Love with its Joy is accompanied, at times, by the vibrant living Youth. The Youth within, is not the Presence within. Youth is jubilant and carefree. Calm is subtle and pure—unaffected. The Presence abides with the Calm. Calm frequently

## A Tiny But Radiant Light

pulsates lightly. The Youth bubbles, is jubilant and exudes massive amounts of energy.

Although these gifts have been known from *Evening One*, while working on September 12, 2008, it suddenly occurred to me that "These are the five proficiencies": Knowledge Known, coexistent with Eternal Life; Calm—perceived as a light weight, but recognized as an intelligible Presence; the Love; the Joy with its accompaniment, Youth.

### Poetry in Delight of Vibrant Youth

#### Youth Born Arising

*In this lingering long,*
*In this outward living,*
*In this thing thinking on,*

*In its laughter exclaiming,*
*In its joyhood proclaiming,*
*In my wonderment exploring,*

*I see, or think I see, believe*
*To be, another spring, a sprig,*
*A twig, a sprout, a youth arising.*

*The babe of laughter, pure delight,*
*A separate living in its childhood,*
*A separate living in its own eyesight,*
*Awake unto itself, acknowledging itself,*
*Perpetual youth, the youth of Youth arising,*

*Within the inward peeping through,*
*With slightly open lids unto the outward,*
*Just sufficient to flash a glimpse to see,*
*To be, to peer unto, to latch unto, to live,*
*Between its youthful, sleeping, restful lids,*
*To live within and now, within the outward too,*

## Margaret Mary Stender

*A teasing, a playing toyfully—Joyousness*
*Eradicating, even in his youth, my control*
*Waylaying me joyfully, playfully, and me*
*In wonderment observing, a playing too.*
   *3/5/1996 TGS*

*O Wondrous Child* and *Yet You Stayed, O Loyalty* appear in the Appendix.

# CHAPTER IV
## Endnotes

Endnote 1
The reference to "Virgin Sophia, i.e. Wisdom," is credited to the use of the word *Sophia* in *The Works of Jacob Behmen*, The Teutonic Theosopher, Volume the Fourth, *The Way To Christ*, Discovered and Described In The Following Treatise: I. *Of True Repentance*. Printed for G. Robinson, in Pater-noster Row. MDCCLXXXI. Herein, Sophia is also accounted as eternal love.

Endnote 2
It is essential to stress that the "flare," when mentioned with the enkindling, only flashes upward. The "traveling" or "momentum" with its physical sensation, is upward, outward, and downward.

This is an exceedingly interesting point to the curious self-consciousness mind: the recognition of the existence of the *top of the head*, is the sole comprehension of any *exterior* object (yet, it is not recognized to be exterior); still it is recognized interiorly. Neither is there the memory of the sight, sound or any other thought pertaining to the outward physical senses during the entire period, from the onset of the winds breaking through the darkness, through the calamitous reawakening to normal consciousness.

On January 12, 2010, during the proofreading of this manuscript, at age seventy-one, it occurred to me that it may be essential to reiterate that, when the flash flared above the head, the physical pulsation was felt and perceived in an identical manner to its perception within the boundary of the physical body. Simultaneously, astonishingly, there was an awareness, a consciousness within the distance. One immediately recognizes the additional distance to be part of oneself.

Endnote 3
*Towards Democracy*, Edward Carpenter. Complete Edition in Four Parts, Published by George Allen and Unwin Limited, at 40 Museum Street, London, W. C., And by S. Clarke Limited, at 41, Granby Row,

Manchester, 1916. *Towards Democracy* will also be found in the public domain on the Internet.

Endnote 4
 Ibid., Part I, XLIII, p 64.
Note the similarity of recognition, with Carpenter's use of the term "disentanglement," and this writer's recognition of a "distancing" to the natural world.

Endnote 5
 Ibid., Part I, LII, pp 82, 83

Endnote 6
 Ibid., Part I, LIX, p 94

Endnote 7
 Ibid., Part I, LXV, pp 103-105

Endnote 8
 Bucke, Richard Maurice, M.D., *Cosmic Consciousness*, New York, E.P. Dutton and Company, Inc., Publishers, Fourteenth Edition, 1948, p 204

Endnote 9
 *Balzac Honore de. A Memoir of,* by K.P. Wormly, Roberts Bros., Boston, 1892, p 5.

## CHAPTER V

## GENERATION—Gifts—Succeeding the Evening and Moment

Subsequent to the evening of 1991, and the preeminent emergence of the five gifts, on September 28, 1992, an ennobling vision emerged. The vision flared, blazed, into existence. The suddenness and clarity amazed me from sleep. Sheer awe abounded. A record of the vision took place immediately with the intention to ensure that the vividness would remain distinct and as crystal clear as the vision itself. Shortly thereafter, the lines were restructured into the semblance of the format of a poem, though the tone remained harsh and stilted, merely functional, as if it were an informational report, which is precisely what it constituted.

Now, why, I do not know. I do not recall why it was structured as a poem with a title. I had never been drawn to write poetry. This event took place roughly two years prior to the unexpected onset of the inspired poetry of 1994, contained herein.

On November 28, 1992, under similar circumstances, I awoke to record the words, *Behold the Daybreak*. Later, by virtue of an error by the publisher, *Behold the Daybreak* became the title of the first book of poetry. In May 1994, there was another vision imparting an emboldened message. Consistent with the message, the poem was titled *Embodiment of Harmony*. This powerful vision is of the highest magnitude and is one of the greatest two ever presented to me. It was as if I was being informed, shown in depth, that something sublime had taken place three years earlier, and, at least in part, I had not consciously recognized the full magnitude of the significance of the enkindling. (Endnote 1)

## Margaret Mary Stender

I assumed that I had, of course. One could not overlook the preeminent fact that in an instant all aspects of my life changed: thoughts; perspective; outlook; physical well-being; demeanor; including the receipt of a sacred knowledge. All aspects were kept secretly treasured until far into the future; they came to light only with the onset of the poetry.

The vision also conveyed the explicit knowledge that the nearly impenetrable barrier—that I had hoped to breach (yet, did not breach at that time, in about 1970, when suffering so dearly over the loss of my mother)—had indeed been breached with the enkindling. Albeit, perchance, comparatively speaking it had been breached as a glance, still as a grand gift, and not of my own making.

A lengthy continuation from *Megan's Story* portrays it clearly.

*Now, hear the sorrowful tale of foolish Megan,*
*Hear the truth of the gifts,*
*Yet hear of the truth of the gifts, of the gift of the presence,*
*That left her in its absence, partial absence, with:*

*First recall the poem, Love the World Doth Own*
*Was this a foreknowledge, a portend,*
*Of the gift, the poetry, to come?*

*—And Meg as she reads, the poetry to perceive, and feel, a minor remnant and reminder of her lost love, her Love Across the Boundary (Whitman), she slightly hears the pulsation in her ears and head, undescribable, and feels throughout the upper of her body a resonance, the sound, or thought of words, rhythmic, a cause to her body to reverberate, a soothing pleasure, a calmness, peacefulness, serenity descends upon her and pervades her. Megan is enveloped in a pleasant aura of contentedness;*

*—A second sight and rarely yet a second double hearing, the heartbeat of her eternal love along beside the heartbeat of Megan loud and clear where within was never either heard before;*

# A Tiny But Radiant Light

*—Unknown to Megan at the time the truth of what it meant. Another vision to her was given and obediently recorded. A little stilted, yet recorded in faithfulness and trust. To her is known as The Veil Is Rent.*

### The Veil is Rent
*Near midnight,*
*A stark pinpoint of radiant white light,*
*Suddenly, burst through the darkness—*
*The brightest light I'd ever "seen."*
*It flared into a small multi-faceted star,*
*The shape of a compass rose.*
*Then flared,*
*In a single, exceedingly thin flash,*
*To the top and to the bottom of my awareness,*

*Then, flared to each side.*
*The dazzling light was ultra-bright,*
*Yet shown only in itself.*
*It did not dissipate,*
*The balance of the darkness.*

*It stood as a cross,*
*With the faceted flare,*
*At the normal level,*
*Of the horizontal arm,*
*Of a cross—*
*The level of the heart of man.*

*The flare took the place,*
*Of the vertical and horizontal,*
*Arms of a cross.*
*It stood erect and shown intensely,*
*Boldly, in the midnight darkness,*
*Splitting and parting the darkness.*

*It was presented to me,*
*"The veil is rent."*
9/2/1992

## Margaret Mary Stender

*—Megan again in 11/92 in intensity of light as Sunday afternoon, appeared as night, saw again, again, and once again, a light appearing as within a dream. And later was a sentence given, Behold the Daybreak.*

*—And,*
*During a night in May of '94, when resistance was diminished, a coming through and known to be to her, to her conscious mind, a vision of a truth where upon awaking she to herself recorded:*

> *"I at a distance, existing only as vision, awareness and knowledge observed, or was shown, what appeared to be many heavenly bodies, orbs, or planets, all moving in infinite silence, harmony, unity, not around a central object, but the totality was circular and space extended beyond the orbs and space. The space or background was black and the orbs were white, my awareness was at an immense distance."*

Which Megan, with her spark, absorbed,
Later translated into a poem of poetry which she called,
Embodiment of Harmony, which you shall view in full below.

### Embodiment of Harmony
*Step back a pace, more likely near a space to peer,*
*Within the deepest depth a distance to perceive,*
*As you the vision the awareness and knowledge,*
*Observe the heavenly bodies, orbs, planets,*
*All moving in infinite silence, harmony.*

*Not around a central core—all the central core,*
*Still moving circling, orbiting, in accord.*

*Observe and feel the peace interior in you,*
*When in the view you view the moving unity,*
*Wisdom, beauty, with each its own rhythm paced,*
*Though with care a rhythm superior to bear.*

*Thus in still peace separately within their sphere,*
*Too, a whole uniting, solitary,*
*A collective universe of mobility.*

## A Tiny But Radiant Light

*See the scene circular and space extends beyond,*
*The shining orbs all lit within the dark of space,*
*As with light that shines from without withon the orbs,*
*Not otherwise light to shine upon the darkness.*

*The deepest dark within itself still stands alone,*
*Forming the body of depth, support for the orbs.*
*Perceived the vision felt and known does not portray,*
*Whereas is the embodiment of harmony, calm, peace.*
*12/4/1994*

*Megan knew that there was, "No question that she was different*
*from that point on. Not better, holier, or more sacred,*
         *Just different..."*

*...Now this our Megan attempted to write.*
*Too, she knew, the gift belonged to others.*
*And she knew, if this, and each his/her gift(s), be given,*
         *be spread worldly-wide,*
*Then retain them, which is tough,*
*There would be mere selflessness.*

*There neither could nor would be war, no famine, no argument,*
*No selfishness, all good would be given away to help another.*
*Imagine a world of givers as opposed to takers? No crime,*
*No condemnation, a mere rejoicing in the abilities,*
*And laughter of another.*

*Into her mind, Megan now knew she knew,*
*And goes on to quietly say, "There are*
*Two centers in the body, in the center middle, and*
*Through poetry, though rhythm, or another way,*
*This, it activates itself with no foretelling*
*Or forewarning it bursts and sheds the dark of*
*Night and illuminates the day. And, it travels.*

*This truth, is not from me, still through me*
*To you: The peak or apex of the height of feeling*
*Leaves a priceless gift, a contentedness, a long term peace,*
*A soothing calm, a satiety beyond compare, no words can*

Margaret Mary Stender

*Describe. Other gifts are left and felt, and sight and sound."*
*(Here stands the end to the selections of Megan's Story)*

## Poetry—Desire, Necessity to Express

On June 3, 1994, or close to three years after the evening of the mystical experience, the poetry actually began. Prior to this day, the only poetry or rhythmic verse involved in my life was incurred by virtue of reading *Leaves of Grass* and by virtue of the evening and moment with the subsequent recording of the few highborn words, which presented themselves either visibly or audibly during sleep, and which are recorded above in *Megan's Story*.

Common everyday poetry, if one can call poetry *common every day*, presented itself to the active mind in a normal rational manner, as a result of an endeavor to address a purely mundane matter. A friend paid a compliment. There was nothing more than a sincere desire to respond with poetry, as the poetry would speak in this person's own inherent language. In the prolonged fervent struggle to respond in like-kind, a rhythm had been found, not a rhyme, not true pure poetry, but a rhythm—the Inward rhythm.

I struggled and struggled to make the poem perfect, yet it was not. Perhaps, it was not even a poem. Nevertheless, it was the affirmative beginning. A fluent-potential blossomed into conscious panoramic view. Here was a manner in which the bounty of the enkindling could be handled: short and succinct; one concept; one emotion; one desire, faculty or attribute, at a time; entirely manageable via the inner rhythm standing-staunch to express itself in the outer world. The gift of love and peace was to be expressed in poetry!

With the instilled rhythm once secured, the words presented themselves near automatically, co-creatively. Herein stood the artistry to pass the knowledge of the mystical experience on.

While still in the newness of the first several months, the lengthy questioning-knowing, *Happiness is Flowing Out*, flowed out.

## A Tiny But Radiant Light

### Selection from *Happiness is Flowing Out*

*The poetry has so many truths,*
  *While yet, I do not view in totality.*
*Currently the feeling, belief, that the ability poetry*
  *could take control if it so desired, and maybe has.*
*Apparently, it and me mutually benefit. Apparently*
  *we form one united whole.*
*If that is true then others do as well.*
  *Which brings us full to the circle, that ultimately*
    *we are one,*
*From one original, from one ground, one ability, one life,*
  *one love, one family,*
*United under the earthly surface far beyond our senses,*
  *beyond current earthly ability to perceive generally,*
*Except a few, and those times brief in passing,*
  *recognized as coincidence rather than reality.*
    *11/11/1994*

With abundant gratefulness, the writing was all consuming, powerful, enthusiastic and non-stopping. Writing engulfed me; usurped all the available hours, and also what previously had been, unavailable hours, day and night. Never has there been such a prolific abundance of buoyant youthful energy companioned with a super-fluency of words, as of a long pent stream suddenly and miraculously released, surging exponentially and flowing. The poetry usurped the entire being. In 1995, the rhythm was to be acknowledged in the following manner.

### Selection from *Spirit of Affinity*

*A rhythm never known before, was to be unbound*
*When once the chord was struck, and once the laughter found.*
  *11/1/1995 TGS*

The poetry was quickly recognized as another gift, albeit a gift of a distinct difference. Formerly the gifts were granted with no exertion on *my* part; they made themselves prominent and available. I should say, "They pronounced themselves." They extended the inner being with the Knowledge, the Calm, the Love, and the offspring; each combined with or augmented the limited natural *abilities*, formed a composite, and grew and thrived.

The magnitude of the illumination, enlightenment, experience, as defined by Bucke, may not wholly be laid claim, but there was "something;" an acknowledged kinship, and wellborn; perhaps, it should be termed embrightenment.

It appears that an *outward* gift such as the rhythmic poetry, may or may not be hidden in abeyance. And that an individual may only recognize its availability when he or she *inadvertently* seeks it, desires it, or more likely when there is the strong inner compulsion, or need, to actually utilize its advantage (Undoubtedly, this is true with other attributes, associated with the five gifts, those of which I am not aware).

Then with a meager attempt on the part of the recipient, a magnanimous gift sprouts into luxurious growth. After commencement, with the accompanying exuberance and energy, one suddenly recognizes the appropriate relationship and the necessity (Endnote 2) for its emergence.

\*\*\*

After the evening and moment of 1991, and prior to the onset of the latent gift of the poetry in 1994, there was a scanty attempt to write about Walt Whitman, my near hero. Although, within a brief period, it was apparent that a straightforward narrative was not in sight, especially a complicated subject such as this popular American icon. I simply did not have the ability. Albeit, because of the unique mild inward rhythm, initially absorbed by virtue of reading Whitman's poetry, to my grateful mind, writing of Whitman was of extreme importance. I also knew that this particular writing, writing *about* Whitman, did not immediately address the weighty topic at hand.

Of course, as another excuse to lay the Whitman venture aside, I was also aware that at least four voluminous volumes, all based

## A Tiny But Radiant Light

upon Horace Traubel's long-term friendship with his friend, Walt Whitman, and his frequent visits to Whitman's home, were still available. Why was I to think that I could write, to speak, or to strike a subject not already dealt with heartily?

Nonetheless, I believed that I must bring his influence into renewed light, to acknowledge what I perceived to be the tremendous benefit ensconced in his work. After all, the lingering-feeling induced by Whitman's rhythm when reading his work over a prolonged period, is, in part, responsible for the instigation in the early evening of the astounding event highlighted herein. The highborn spontaneous embrightenment-enlightenment experience is primal; available to all, though relatively uncommon. Whitman is definitely my earthborn mentor.

Although unable to write about Whitman, still I hungered to write and seemed compelled to write about him, and, at that point, after the evening and prior to the onset of the poetry, I was still completely silent about my personal experience. (There is the initial interlude of quietude, of staying solely within oneself.)

I never thought of myself as a poet, nor had an inclination to become one. But now, now after the onset of the poetry, "my" poetry, I consider myself to be *his poet*, one of the poets to come; one of the poets, he knew was to come.

### POETS TO COME (Endnote 3)

*Poets to come! Orators, singers, musicians to come!*
*Not to-day is to justify me and answer what I am for,*
*But you, a new brood, native, athletic, continental, greater than*
  *before known,*
*Arouse! For you must justify me.*

*I myself but write one or two indicative words for the future,*
*I but advance a moment only to wheel and hurry back in the*
*darkness.*

*I am a man who, sauntering along without fully stopping, turns*
  *a casual look upon you and then averts his face,*

## Margaret Mary Stender

*Leaving it to you to prove and define it,*
*Expecting the main things from you.*

With exuberance, in the first eighteen months after the initiation of the poetry, both *The Silent Sound and In Prophet's Truth*, later, known as *Behold the Daybreak* was written and later published under a *pseudonym*; my given name. In several additional months, *In Prophet's Travel* with *Crown of Pearl*, renamed *The Green Springing*, was written. The truly astonishing aspect of the writing was that the gift of the Love and of the Calm brought to bear, or begot, the insight, the inspiration, the content, and their/its own windfall of energy. The poetry was generated from the radiant-within, shining and glowing into the without—into the outward world.

When the emotions are at their passion, the writing is easy, unduly straightforward, sprung-out-brazen, alive, riding the crest of the wave. At those times, the self-conscious mind does not care nor consider how maudlin or overly emotional the work may sound. What one writes is what one is. Writing is fast, simple in context, and near automatic. With only an initial sense of direction, the poem seems to race forward to complete itself.

The writing flows freely in concert with the inborn rhythm and the result bears a cadence, synchronized with the pulsation mildly gyrating—in accordance with the calm—in the body and head during its composition. Under these conditions, a duel meaning (one is always conscious of the two-fold meaning) is frequently carried as a shining spiritual thread; a golden truth, revealed beneath the commonplace language and meaning. The writer comprehends that over a prolonged period, the rhythm will be perceived inwardly and conveyed to a dedicated reader.

The following poem, vision, was written to exemplify the inner rhythm:

Wind Takes Its Rush, but Leaves Its Hush Behind
—A Vision

*This woman again was seen,*
*along the flighting path,*

## A Tiny But Radiant Light

*Flighting, briskly, swiftly, speeding,*
        *borne by the dashing ravishing winds*
*As two lengths of her long filmy long*
        *silky long portending scarf wafts*
*Protracted and horizontal trailing,*
        *in the breeze behind her,*

*As mildly quavering, as pulses*
        *in agreement with breezes,*
*Brusque and hush within—And mild*
        *and wild as breezes race,*

*Envision in, within, mind's eye,*
        *(winds) as flaming ravishing flames,*
*Forsooth, as lying on one side, enforce*
        *or substantiate within the mind.*

*For though the breezes seem blind,*
        *—invisible to the eye*
*—As they have disappeared from view,*
        *within mind lies still the portrait*
*Of wind-blowing force and aptitude and path,*
        *—if one besets his mind to see, envision,*
*As above, the flame lying blazing, forthright,*
        *horizontal, lying on its side, flaming,*
*As from a supine position, a blazing, generally,*
        *thence forward, with laps or laves of flame.*

*Flaming, (wind-ing) flapping, cracking, sounding, pulsing,*
        *causing, creating, pulse, the beat and then relent,*
*To gyrate forth and back, the sortie—one way and back.*
        *The rush then hush equal to the pulse—a pulse,*

*Then within and around and about the corresponding other,*
        *the rush then hush attune—the pulse or flutter,*
*Then as the flame or breeze relents, abates, disappears,*
        *it takes its rush, but leaves its hush behind.*
        *3/14/1998 TFE*

Margaret Mary Stender

Visions—The Living Life Within the Living Life

Again, I descend into personal history, history in the shallow depths.

It is a massive undertaking for a non-writer to even hope to compose a sensible document which would accurately address the emotional, physical, and especially the spiritual magnitude and upheaval of the event delineated herein. Each gift granted possesses its own independent or dependent mode of birth or entrance, immediate with the enkindling, delayed, or as the outgrowth from another: its bourgeoning, magnitude, and progression; its duration of active life-cycle, including the perpetual crest and trough, action and interaction, and rest.

Lengthy deliberation eventually culminated in the development of a huge preliminary table of contents which included a large quantity of poetry. Each poem stressed or alluded to one or more pertinent points, which were currently in possession and dominated, or at least influenced, the thought, perspective and behavior, and each poem generally afforded a semblance of a reference to a period of activity of a gift.

Although, once the initial chronology of the experience was set forth, except for the much later reduction in the all-too-elaborate and cumbersome initial plan for the second half of the book, the outline of the first part of the book essentially remained intact. The only present concern while writing this narrative is still to assure that the chronology is accurate and the chronology is vaguely elusive. (Endnote 4) The experience itself is integral and remains clearly in focus. The gifts are coexistent with the being.

Eventually, it became apparent that the section on Visions should precede the section on the Detrimental Decline as the visions are kin to the initial aspects of the evening and moment; yet visions are especially coexistent with the late emerging poetry.

In some measure, it is also plausible to set the section on the Detrimental Decline prior to the section on Visions, as the loss or reduction of the gifts—the clearly apparent declination of the Perpetual Calm and the Noble Love—was solely responsible for the detrimental decline; indeed, the multitude of the increasing prophetic visions held sway over the period of the decline.

By coincidence, the latter days of the decrease of the gifts coincided with an exceptionally troubling period in my personal life. After several months of perilous duress, the prophetic visions with their commanding reassurance uplifted and propelled me miraculously over the hurdle. They abolished the significant stress and worry as they assured a favorable outcome regarding two strenuous situations.

The visions also forewarned of other rough regions to come and of their short duration. Benevolent visions arose from the deep interior, while selfish entreaties for the full-surge-return of the "lost" gifts sprang from me. Nonetheless, decline or no decline, a mild underlying or composed-passive joy endured.

This contradiction is incomprehensible to the conscious mind, but true. Entreaties for the return of the gifts in their grand magnitude persisted throughout the period of the detrimental decline. Nevertheless, there remained a joy and a knowledge embedded within the underlying knowledge of a divine influence looking-out and clearing the path ahead.

*Alight the Night with Daybright* appears in the Appendix.

\*\*\*

As we each know, there is a marked impressive difference between a mere dream and a prophetic vision. Everyone is familiar with the proverbial dream and there appears to be a common understanding of the definition. The word "dream" generally needs no further elaboration.

My personal opinion is that every adult has also had at least one authentic enlightening, or prophetic vision. The term "vision" as defined in this work, without the proverbial shred of a doubt, constitutes a clarity; it is clear and concise. It gives rise to at least one dynamic color. Moreover, the vision embodies one or more of the following characteristics or conditions.

Visions:
> —Usher in an accompanying sound or sounds which may or may not flutter, quiver, or vibrate giving rise to a rhythm or pulsation which affects the physical body, and induces the body to reverberate with the selfsame frequency. This rhythmic-frequency occurs during the vision and also extends into the wholly awakened state, thence tarries up to many hours, imposing a melodious quality of life;
> —Cause one to expressly hear words spoken, sounding as if heard by the outward ear;
> —Awaken the intellect to an alternative level of consciousness;
> —Incorporate the individual as a "participant," or as both the participant and the "observer";
> —Occasionally convey a cognition belonging to, or commonly associated with the *Divine*;
> —Reveal regions unknown and unavailable to the physical human eye;
> —Afford previously unknown knowledge;
> —Portend to the present or future, or forewarn with an outcome;
> —Convey a clear understanding of meaning and purpose; its own message, interpretation and understanding;
> —Serve the individual in wonderful untold ways;
> —Etch themselves nearly photographically into the mind and memory; and,
> —Undoubtedly, there are several additional valid characteristics.

Beyond this brief general outline of characteristics, the exact nature and the ultimate origin of the visions appear unfathomable. True visions arise from the *depths*, register, bestow their proffer of guidance or intuitive knowledge at their own discretion or will. Commission completed, they relent to the surface-depths of the memory. Visions also create an earnest desire to remember or to record; to affirmatively retain; visions recognize themselves to be relevant.

True visions extend far beyond the scope or the need of the personal ego (a self-satisfaction at one's *achievement*), and ego should not be permitted to enter in. There should be no "self-aggrandizement." Visions are engifted and bear no achievement or credit of one's own.

Herein, a huge percentage of the visions were afforded in radiant vibrant color, and registered a singular knowledge previously unknown to the conscious mind. One grand example is the view of the underlying Golden Glow.

Visions strengthen, encourage, augment, and invaluably lighten the spiritual pathway. I assert, these have been timely, of a particular advantage, and the majority have been diligently and faithfully recorded, albeit frequently in a somewhat rhythmic manner.

And, interesting, even to me, the conscious mind me, the consciousness in relating certain aspects in this overall work, indiscriminately frequently elects to change from the first person to the third person. I am perplexed. There seems to be no valid explanation for the shift in this perspective. I let it stand.

At any rate, the intention is not to dwell upon the all-encompassing definition of Visions, but to provide a foundation with which to work. It is the hope to let the poetry simply speak for itself, to offer the reader an opportunity to evaluate each precise vision, as-well-as to determine whether it carries an immediate-personal or a universal message. Many were designed to assist or guide in day-by-day life.

Other visions portend to the near or far future, even onto Eternity. A few point to, bear witness to, or provide evidence of a Love—Eternal, better known as a Life Everlasting. This, of course, you the reader will discern and decide for yourself. Only a smidgeon of the actual number of visions is presented herein.

Possibly, the overriding message is to realize that when sought in earnest, a peep into the supernal world is accessible to each of us via our own unique manner, in our own especial time.

The prolific period for visions inclined toward June 1997, provided a steady stream through 1998, and declined in 1999 through about February 2000: thereafter, visions appeared only rarely. They rose to a peak during the writing of the second and especially the third book, *The Forever Entwined;* a book seeming to sob unabashed over the decline of the gifts; it encompasses a great deal of what appears now to be an unnecessarily prolonged period of lamentation. Obviously, it was legitimate and sincere for its time.

One morning in 2003, a vision ascended in full dramatic implication: *I Was Given the Fourth!* It was clearly presented that another book is forthcoming. Even in the deepest recesses of my mind, I could not fathom another book. Still, the *Speaking of Itself*—as I describe the interior conveyance—had spoken. I could not doubt this vision; I knew better!

Thinking in retrospect, I simply could not entertain the thought of writing in the manner which I believed it must be written, a straightforward report. Eventually, I began to develop a concept for an Internet Web site. Although, in spite of the vision—the directive—little consideration had been given to actually writing another book. There was also no further desire to write poetry. In fact, every distinguishing feature regarding the evening in 1991 and the resulting events had already come to print in the poetry. (Endnote 5)

Work for a computer website did intrigue me. Development lasted roughly three months. In about mid-July of 2005, the desire to develop a website dramatically changed and the website material was expanded with an eye toward developing a book! (This was expounded upon somewhat, in an earlier section.)

After a brief period I—the conscious-mind "I"—quit! The massive undertaking was overwhelming, and, in this instance, the conscious mind adamantly intermittently *dug in its heels* and resisted. I realized this book was not to be written near automatically as the majority of the poetry had been, but it must receive serious "left brain" consideration, and planning; a task which I now wished to achieve, yet I knew my meager writing skills would thwart.

## A Tiny But Radiant Light

Two years later, with the continual inner prompting, there re-arose the compelling desire to speak "aloud" once again. The writing resumed. Shortly, therein, I quit for a period of several months. I quit several times and there were prolonged periods in between. Since the book remained active in my mind and by then heavily on my *conscience,* I eventually reduced the initial scope of the second half to what I considered possibly to be manageable and began once again. The object of the vision, *Given the Fourth,* is this resultant tiny light.

### Poetry in Honor of the Prophetic Visions

### Given the Fourth

*Because I had three in plain view,*
    *I was given the fourth.*
*Because I had three which no one had seen,*
    *I was given the fourth.*

*Dumbfounded, astounded, given to mind,*
    *I wondered in doubt*
*As another did too, was there again three in number*
    *hidden from all view?*

*I checked in the vision: Two were stuck relatively tight.*
    *Yet, there was one plus the two,*
*Making Three. And, because there were three,*
    *I was given the fourth.*
        *11/27/2003, Thanksgiving Day*

### Sun Appeared with Motion Teeming

*The blazon white sun appeared within the lower hemisphere,*
    *slightly barely toward the West inches above*
        *the horizon.*
*Then the conscious mind—a-gawk at blazon ultra-white*
    *with motion teeming interior—it noticed*

## Margaret Mary Stender

*The slim and slender rays, so fine and thin, spectacular,*
    *—plenipotentiary, multi floral, delicate, superior.*

*The sun, the white, enhanced itself to flaming ultra-white,*
    *and the eyes they feared of sight with the gazing,*
*But the mind, the superior mind, it knew the gazing*
    *would not harm, for the sight was of itself interior,*

*Far beyond the reach of the earthly careless eyes, and so*
    *it gazed, it praised and gawked, it drank within*
        *the depths,*
*It absorbed the rays, or splendor of, and rests, now rests*
    *in peace, serenity, and calm.*
        *3/7/1998 TFE*

## To Breach the Gap—You Are the Living Life Within the Living Life

Occasionally in life, it is essential to step aside from one's immediate intention and insert a bubble, or a parenthesis of a sort, to address a critical issue or situation. Each of us is familiar with this type of near-daily redirection of activity. In this instance, in this writing, and since this week's unexpected related event is similar in nature to what is being described in this narrative, it is appropriate to insert a few descriptive paragraphs regarding a recent vision and past visions which initially I had not intended to include. They purport to the same *end*—Eternal life.

During the night of June 17, 2008, I was jolted awake with the solitary word "Ira." Instantly, I knew that my friend Ira, age 84, had died and that I had been *informed*. Infused within the vision was the recognition that he is alright. *Alright* is strange and vague, and I cannot pretend to know exactly what it means. Still, in one word I was told of his death, and of his *Life*. In some remote manner, I was informed that he still lives and that he is concerned, or at a minimum that he is "thinking" of me; not of

## A Tiny But Radiant Light

himself; not of his own death; but of alerting me; of reaching *out* to me.

On this particular morning, the morning of Ira's death, I was unconscionably weary. This is nearly unheard of for me. I am a distinct morning person. I knew that he had died.

The previous day, I contemplated going to North Carolina or to the Diamond Crater in Arkansas to dig for gemstones. However, today, I awoke knowing that I must stay in Batesville and wait for the dreaded telephone call.

Finally, while getting out of the bathtub, the telephone rang. It was Ira's daughter, saying, "Peg, I have bad news." Without realizing what I was saying I silently whispered, "I know." His daughter said that he had died in his sleep at 5:29 a.m. that morning. I was aware of keeping her on the telephone too long under the circumstances, though it was only about two minutes. It seemed that I could hold on to my friend a little longer. I did not tell her of the vision.

In order to effectively explain the profound effects of this current audible one word *vision* and the surrounding circumstances concerning Ira, I must also relate two momentous visions concerning my father. These are visions which occurred five years, and also approximately eight to ten years, earlier. These two are visions of which, prior to Ira's death and the immediate recognition of a certain similarity, I was not previously planning to relate.

I will begin with the second vision first: In the dark of the night, in sleep or near sleep, on September 16, 2003, a name presented itself to me with the distinct and audible interior words "Everett Stender," my father's name. The words awoke me with a start as if they had also been heard by virtue of the external ear. Instantly I knew and understood the message; the message of eternal life; the meaning, "I want you to know, I am *living*; I am well; I now understand."

This vision was so profound, so invigorating, and so welcome with its pure knowledge that Dad was all right and that he had intentionally communicated his position directly to me, that the only immediate question in my mind, which incredulously astounds me even today, was "Why was the name 'Everett' Stender given rather than the name 'Bud'?" Everyone had always called my dad by his nickname, Bud or Buddy. Then I realized, he is Everett Stender, not Bud Stender.

By this vision, I knew that my father had finally found the appropriate "mood" or state of my mind, or state of my being (understanding lapses here), or *method* which permitted him to breach the gap, to alert me to his awareness and life. Dad died on July 1, 2003, but communicated three and one-half months later.

Here are the pertinent circumstances surrounding his death and my forewarned knowledge.

Several years prior to my dad's death, by virtue of a vision, I was made aware of the scene that I was to see in the physical world just prior to his death. I knew that when I saw that particular setting, it would be the final time that I would see my father alive, incredible, but true. A few years later, on June 30, it happened. I experienced the setting. I recognized it. My face reflected the devastating impact of the memory of the prophetic vision. Dad, in turn, recognized that something was drastically wrong in my stare and openmouthed look. He responded in a peculiar way. Then, I responded in an equally peculiar way.

He said, "Good Bye." In an endeavor to understand my horrified look, he struggled and hesitated strangely between the Good and the Bye; he spoke in an abnormal high-pitched voice, I responded with the identical off-tone and hesitant stumbling Good and the delayed Bye. Stunned: in disbelief, I turned to walk into the house.

Then, the thought occurred to me that I would be able to see him again if I turned back around to see him drive out of the circular drive. To my naïve astonishment, he was not driving. He was on the passenger side, and with the sun reflecting precisely in the wrong location, I could not distinguish him. I did not see him.

I refused to admit the verity of the vision. I adamantly argued with myself. I talked myself out of believing that this would be the final time I would see him. I convinced myself, and was firmly adamant that I *would* see him again! In stubborn disbelief,

# A Tiny But Radiant Light

I left town. I was indeed alerted via the vision, but I did not see him again. The following morning, I learned of Dad's death.

I will conclude with a happy ending, anyway. In addition to the normal turmoil at the death of a loved one, I struggled mightily for nearly three months; not because I denied the vision; not because I knew better; not because I had left town, but because I tortured myself as a result of the manner in which dad and I had said "Goodbye." I knew that he knew that something was dreadfully wrong. I knew that the long drawn out goodbye was due to the quizzical, non-understanding, look he gave me, while intently observing "my non-wanting" to believe in what I knew to be true—my comprehending vacant stare." My look was the cause for his awkward interrupted goodbye.

After his death, that goodbye meant to me that I would literally *never* see him again. (During his lifetime, my dad never said goodbye, he always said, so long.) It troubled me beyond despair. Goodbye, in this instance, where he actually said goodbye and where I had seen the vision beforehand, was interpreted to mean "finite," no eternal life. The exaggerated Goodbye clouded all of my beliefs; caused me to question my understanding—my true knowing—of eternal life.

After nearly three months, troubled beyond discretion, I finally told his wife the situation, and about being sorely disturbed over the Goodbye. She immediately sat straight up and said, "After we left, your dad said 'Why did I say goodbye, I should not have said goodbye.'" My heart leaped in relief and understanding. I *would* see him again. We should not have said goodbye after all: he wholly understood that we should not have said goodbye. There was no finality after all.

There is one more essential component of these two similar situations which should be told. During the early morning of Ira's death when I was so exceedingly weary, not tired, but weary, I clearly understood that this was the same weariness I had experienced once before. The initial overpowering weariness lasted for several hours while I was driving to Batesville, Arkansas, in 2003, to visit my daughter. Even then while driving,

## Margaret Mary Stender

I knew this was a strange unexplainable heavy imposing weariness, nearly unbearable, but I knew not its cause.

I repeatedly questioned its source, but I could not understand. What I did not know was that the weariness began about the time of my father's accident and death, but before I had been informed by my husband. I was driving unknowingly in the weariness of death. Now, in the morning prior to being informed of Ira's death by his daughter, the recognizable heavy weariness was being re-experienced.

### Golden Glow—The Wonderment

As proclaimed numerous times, to varying degrees splendid gifts have been granted as a result of the embrightenment experience, meaning the gifts incurred as a result of the mystical revelation. Before that evening and night in July 1991, I was only aware of the sparse potential for an experience similar to this in nature.

Now, having *lived conjointly* with the abiding revelation's offspring in the regular workaday world for roughly seventeen years, this writer is confident to identify and verify the existence and the virtue of certain facets of living life, herein brought to light.

There is, however, one revelation, derived in succeeding years, which does not appear to have a distinctive reference in the mystical works of antiquity, at least in the form similar to which I have been exposed and able to observe. It was made known through the veracity of several poignant visions.

Within these visions, the wholly aware perception is allowed either to view a still life scene, or to participate in a scenario encompassing motion which focuses on one superb distinguishing feature. The scenes, pertain either to the birth of a Golden Glow or actually show the golden glow residing within, without, and throughout the scene, throughout nature and beyond. As a point of interest, visions with notable motion are the most potent.

## A Tiny But Radiant Light

In other words, the golden glow underlies and also surmounts, shines forth from all of eternity, and from every material and non-material *thing* or particle. It appears to constitute an undertone, an underlying principle. The visions, including the visions of the golden glow, coexist with their meaning even as the *knowledge known* coexists, united, with the enkindling; even as we, our thought, coexists with our consciousness and activity.

An intriguing point of interest is that when writing of the golden glow, it frequently seems prudent to present it from the male point of view, though it is also known by the finite conscious mind that it should also be presented equally from the female point of view, or from the neutral standpoint.

## Poetry by Virtue of the Hallowed Golden Glow

### Selection from *Joy of Love*

*O the gentle, calming, lulling attribute, the kind, considerate,*
    *peaceful joy—the light, the shining of the ultra-sight,*
*The golden glow surmounting all—under all, just merely*
    *barely—just out of sight.*
    *6/10/1997 TGS*

### Still Wonder Interior to All

*"Dear O Prophet heavenly, sitting near the fire, though,*
    *I know not why, O Prophet, thou ist sitting by thy fire.*
*For 'tis spring and warm and pleasant, mid-spring flowers*
    *near their bloom, early blossoms soothly bursting,*
*Wild ginger, bloodroot, the lily, violet, and daffodil.*
    *Still thou, O Prophet, sitteth idle by thy fire.*

*Thou must be contemplating the burgeoning of the spring,*
    *the fervent warmth of sun, the shine, the purging rain,*
*The blithe and gentle fragrant breeze. Ah, feel that breeze.*
    *Yet thee O Prophet, sitteth by thy mid-evening fire—Or*

## Margaret Mary Stender

*Perhaps O Prophet, thou contemplatest the Eastern hemisphere,*
    *Jupiter and Venus shadowed by the sliver-slice of moon."*
*(And, the Prophet responds:)*
*"O my dear, sitteth thee down and lookest thee around, beyond*
    *the mid-spring flowers, the buds bursting on the trees,*
*See beyond the welcome sun, the sunshine golden blazon streaming,*
    *beyond the Jupiter, the Venus, or the silver crescent moon.*
*O my dear, hear, then strive to see interiorly the limpid glow,*
    *the radiate emerging rising glowing slightly out of sight.*

*"O my dear, the golden glow is everywhere—greets from everywhere,*
    *from the crags and crevices from the deep and vast ravine,*
*From the sky the atmosphere translucent flowing through the boughs*
    *and greens of trees and if it is but once given thee to see,*
*Thee too, forsooth, shall sittest thee with me idle by the fire*
    *contemplating the wonder beyond, beneath, interior to all."*
    *4/14/98 TFE*


## Bubbling Golden, as Ginger Floating
### —A Vision

*A week ago, Sunday, unable to sleep,*
    *arose, reclined on the couch,*
*Read St. Augustine for a couple of hours,*
    *placed the book right on the floor,*
*Slipped eyelids closed and dozed.*

*The wonderment, the wonder-bliss, awakening me,*
    *—partially awakening—awakening the consciousness,*
*The second consciousness to think, to ponder of the pending*
    *wonder, (Endnote 6)*
    *culminating in the rush—bubbling golden, as ginger floating,*
*Frothing, to the top, the apex of the consciousness*
    *—second consciousness—the ultra-sight, ultra-bright, the*
    *delight.*

*The thinking-on, the knowing of the miracle ascending once again,*
    *the inner-sight, astounded by the golden rushing to*
    *the top,*

# A Tiny But Radiant Light

*The long, prolonged duration. Then mildly slightly quavering,
the after-shock, the tempered-tone, the hallowed-
mellowness,
The mind and muscle, fluxing, pulsing, in attune—Relaxed.
Serene, throughout the night, throughout the morn, throughout
the eve.
2/11/2000*

*Alight the Night with Daybright, Dawned the Second Birth*—A Vision, and *The Hallowed Golden Glow*—A Vision, appear in the Appendix.

## Honorè de Balzac, Speaks of the Golden Glow

Above under *Golden Glow—The Wonderment*, written many months ago, you *heard* me say, there is one distinctive revelation which does not appear to have a reference in the mystical works of the past. Still, in September 2008, in rereading *Seraphia* after many years, I came upon a reference in *The Works of Honorè De Balzac (Endnote 7)* where the identical words, "Golden Glow" were used to describe a brilliant splendor, a brilliant countenance. The words "Internal impetus" and "constant presence of an internal glow," caused renewed excitement and an instant recognition.

Balzac, in one of his two most famous works, (Endnote 8) *Seraphita*, spoke of Seraphitus who "shone with such brilliant splendor." Then Balzac asks, "Was the *radiance* due to the effulgence…by the *pure* mountain air and the reflection from the snow? Was it the result of an *internal impetus* which still excites the frame at the moment it is resting after long exertion?" or "Was it produced by the sudden contrast between the *golden glow* of sunshine and the gloom of the clouds through which this pretty pair had passed?"

To my perception, Balzac expressly identifies the true nature of the brilliant splendor as it appears from his distinctive vantage point; he calls it the *golden glow*. He mentions purity, *pure*. He deliberately provides the reader a choice in which to believe, to understand, to internally identify with. He provides a clue, a framework upon which to build. The message is clear. There is an internal impetus, a radiance, a golden glow.

Balzac purposefully elects to further describe Seraphitus "...to judge by the boldness of his brow and the light in his eyes at this moment, was a youth of seventeen." Balzac stresses that if Seraphitus had been seen by another "he would, no doubt, have believed in the existence of a phosphoric fluid in the sinews that seemed to shine through the skin, or in the constant presence of an *internal glow*, which tinted Seraphitus as a light shines through an alabaster vase. ...The *fire that blazed in his eyes* rivaled the rays of the sun; he seemed not to receive but *to give out light*. ...but this absolutely effortless mien was the outcome rather of a mental state than of physical habit." (The italics are mine.)

Let this glimpse into the mind of an exceptional man, an enlightened man, entice you to read Balzac's *Seraphita* in its entirety.

Several months later, two additional pertinent references to the golden glow inadvertently crossed my path. (Endnote 9)

# CHAPTER V
## Endnotes

Endnote 1
The *Embodiment of Harmony* is briefly addressed in the section on Bucke, under Intellectual Illumination.

Endnote 2
An exception to the recognition of the necessity of its delayed emergence, seems solely to be the non-recognition which resounds in the inability for the conscious mind to understand the purpose of the ability of the Youth Within to win a multitude of insignificant drawings. The conscious mind simply has never understood what appears to be the necessity to win those drawings; it believes that it is "taking advantage," wrong. There must be a great underlying creativity which seeks to be expressed, and also seeks to be recognized.

Endnote 3
Walt Whitman, *Leaves of Grass*, Including *Sands at Seventy*...1$^{st}$ Annex, *Good-Bye My Fancy*...2$^{nd}$ Annex, *A Backward Glance O'er Travel'd Roads, and Portrait from Life*. Copyright 1891.

Endnote 4
There was an advantage, although nonchalant and purely mundane, a stroke of good fortune, granted years ago in approximately 1975-76. The, then, Kalamazoo, Michigan, City Manager, Robert Bobb, came to speak to the employees of the Office of the City Treasurer. One of the points that he made was how crucial it is to date everything. That lesson took root and has been utilized conscientiously for the entire balance of my life. Without that pearl of advice, the chronology of the early visions would not have been maintained. I owe him a huge debt of gratitude.

Endnote 5

Except much later, during the writing of the second part of this book, there was the sudden realization that during and subsequent to the evening and moment, one aspect did not particularly stand out. It, the "darkness," had been eclipsed by the enkindling. Not until I began to write about the Subjective Light was the importance of the darkness recognized; the breaking-forth through the darkness (the vertical darkness) with no perceived interval of elapsed time between the breaking-forth, coexistent with the recognition of the raging winds, and when the winds arrived and struck, delivered, the enkindlement.

At that time, credence should also have been given to the darkness, for without the darkness the enkindling could not have been actualized. A further description of this unusual aspect will be found in the second half of this book under Richard Maurice Bucke, M.D., *Marks of Cosmic Sense*, in subsection *Subjective Light*, and under John Middleton Murry, *Comment: Dark/Darkness*. (pages 15-17, 100, 131-132, 144-146)

Endnote 6

At these times, one's consciousness could, in awe, study the vision, consider and evaluate it as it remained visible or occurred—as it presented itself.

Endnote 7

*The Works of Honore De Balzac*, Volume II, containing *Seraphita*, Avil Publishing Company, Philadelphia. Copyright 1901 by John D. Avil, p 14-15.

Endnote 8

*Louis Lambert* (Believed to depict Balzac's personal story) and *Seraphita* are to be found in the public domain on the Internet. (The word Seraphim is associated with an angelic being, with purity, with light.)

Endnote 9

In *The Eagle's Gift*, SIMON AND SCHUSTER, New York, p 230, Carlos Castaneda, in speaking of his benefactor the Nagual Juan Matus, and of Castaneda's counterpart the Nagual woman, during her experience in what Castaneda called the Left Side Attention, or the Second Attention, reports "...the whole room became incandescent; everything glowed with an amber light" and that the amber light resembled fog, and fog became amber cobwebs, and, finally, "the

## A Tiny But Radiant Light

world remained…amber…" Don Juan informed her that the right side of the world was veiled in amber fog, and the left side was clear.

On page 247, Castaneda explains: The right side instruction pertained to the state of normal consciousness and had to do with leading him to the rational conviction there is another type of awareness concealed in human beings. The left side instruction is related to the state of heightened awareness and had to do exclusively with the handling of the second attention.

*The Power of Silence, Further Lessons of Don Juan*, SIMON AND SCHUSTER, p 121, "…second attention—the counterpart of my normal attentiveness."

*Life After Life*, The 25th Anniversary of the Classic Bestseller, by Raymond A. Moody, Jr., M.D. *The Investigation of a Phenomenon—Survival of Bodily Death*, p 68 quotes an interviewee, after their near death experience, as reporting that she was "…moving swiftly…" and from out of the darkness, she proceeded through a gray mist, and that "the whole thing was permeated with…a living, golden yellow glow…"

## CHAPTER VI

## LOSS OF THE COLOSSAL LOVE ETERNAL
## —O My Virgin Sophia

Loss of Love Eternal—Loss of Actively Living as One

The Love Eternal is an elusive concept, and, as near as can be derived represents the totality of the gift, the "Found," the supreme unity—a glowing of love—with its varying facets, emblossomed within. The colossal love eternal—the underlying all-centering entity, a composite, the One; Love Eternal reigns supreme.

When the Calm and, too, the Love, diminish, one's *heart* begins to fracture, then seems to break into a sundry of pieces, inwardly sobs in confusion, feels that it has been betrayed, or has in some manner betrayed itself, and attempts desperately, yet without knowing how, to retrieve or regenerate its lost love.

The entire being is drawn into the loss and pleads for the return of its all-consuming Love; the body, the mind, and the soul quietly mourn and weep. Eventually, the *loss* is so strikingly detrimental that the vacancy is not only reflected in the poetry, but dominates the poetry. It speaks openly unabashed in lamentation. (Endnote 1)

If speaking technically, I blunder in speech. The detrimental decline, the unitary expression of the dreadful feeling is represented as a complete loss, or lost. The term loss or lost is not strictly true—although it feels as if the love and the calm are virtually lost. Perchance, a more descriptive word, as indicated in a few instances, would be a recession, a retreat, or a withdrawal. Even a drawing-back, a recoil, will spring again.

## A Tiny But Radiant Light

No acquired faculty is ever truly lost. All gained supernal knowledge and inspired activity and every inborn attribute is already consolidated in the being with the advent of the enkindling, and that incorporation takes place in the most phenomenal manner: as in a harmonious symphony, an infinity of instruments; alert to its own knowing of itself.

This Love Eternal, although try as hard as I may, I cannot prove it or effectually express it—the Calm appears actually to be conspicuously essential to the Love Eternal—a composite sprouting near or interchangeable affectations; Calm reclines, yet influences and produces. Love flows radiant. Love radiates, glows and flares outward, making one larger than oneself (And that especial Love is accompanied by Love's subtle inward joy—not merely the *flaming* Joy as otherwise propounded herein.) These two, the Calm and the Love, yet interdependent may produce the one, the wave, and, too, the balance of life, for life.

The Calm weighs to one, is united: the Love weighs to one and flares to another, presupposes another, encloses another. The Calm is One. Glowing in love—if one is effectually glowing *with/in* the Eternal Love, Love Eternal—is One.

The Presence may be entirely dependent upon or lives coexistent with the Calm; as the Calm is also, coexistent with the Love. Although, if this does not appear to be contradictory, the Presence does not appear to necessarily be coexistent with the Love. The Presence makes itself felt, known, apparent, and prominent, yet always in conjunction with the Calm. The Calm is as a light weight, as dew is perceived, albeit, generally with a perceptible mild pulsation or quavering. Notwithstanding, the mortal so blessed desires, prefers, the deep possessive Calm.

In spite of everything, for a meritorious time, the faithful joyous Youth within retains a degree of buoyancy to the very *end*. In reality, there is no end. (If I were a writer, this narrative would be less repetitious and more concise, as I believe that it has not been to this point. There would be less appearance of contradiction.)

## Margaret Mary Stender

## Poetry in Outcry of the Declivity of the Colossal Love Eternal

### Light the Light

*Let me back within your shadow*
    *even the shadow of light is bright.*

*Light the light within my heart,*
    *ignite the flame within my breast,*

*Let me bask within Love's shadow,*
    *even the shadow of Love is light.*
        *8/26/1996 TGS*


### For the Absence of its Lily

*After the dawn of day has struck,*
    *is there no conscience or is there no sin?*

*Now what seems to be so long ago and seems to be so far away,*
    *six years or so, of attributes, of gifts, of love, of joy,*
*Of purporting of itself full-fledged, and O of yet, O yet of woe,*
    *of yearning listless unrelenting unrelinquishing heartache,*
*The a-lonesomeness—the missing of the calm—the non-succumbing*
    *wholly to the joy, the quiet laughter, the solemn cheer,*
*The non-relenting fully to the buoyancy, the overwhelming glowing*
    *with frequency, the radiation, the emanation, the ever-flowing*
*Outpouring, outgoing, the floating, the fountain, the fervency,*
    *the love enthralling abounding surrounding and the memory,*

*The union full-fact and truth intact, for the absence of its Sophia,*
    *its wisdom, its blossom, its lily, its blitheful calm.*
        *2/7/1998 TFE*


### Exceed within My Being

*O this, thy Sunday morning,*
    *the heart is lagging fast withon the ground,*

## A Tiny But Radiant Light

*In its mellow tone, in its somewhat dreary,*
      *in its longing lonely after, for the one eternal love alone,*
*The one unto its presence is already known. The one unto eternity,*
      *the only Heavenly One, to wit, from which, was born—was*
      *borne.*

*The Love—the long lasting, long-forever-lasting,*
      *—Thus, the longing, the yearning undertone,*
*The now, the overtone, the yelling, screaming,*
      *silently pleading—for Love's return.*

*O Love, why didst thee show thy brilliant face,*
      *then hide within the haze, the overcast.*
*O Love, thy calm, the lull, the merely quiet,*
      *to my mind must come must dwell anew,*

*Must be and live, exceed, within my being,*
      *and I at now, for thee do pledge,*
*To be thy faithfulness, O Love.*
      *In thy being, thou dost dwell*
*And through thine window thou dost peer,*
      *and unto me thine beams, thy radiant,*
*The beaming comes to be, and O my Love,*
      *my faithfulness, I love thee.*
      *11/17/1996 TGS*


## Bleat, but for Thy Calm

*O love, thou assaultest me—lay me low*
      *—with thine yearning longing,*
*With thy continual pleading, thy earnestness,*
      *thy non-relenting steadfastness,*
*Thy craving nagging hunger,*
      *thy gigantic thirst,*
*Thy unquenched ardor,*
      *thy massive nostalgia,*
*(As thee searchest for what seems*
      *to me to be, thy Holy Grail),*

## Margaret Mary Stender

*For thy Love, thy own Love,*
*    the deep with-inseated still-fullness,*
*        thy liberty, thy clear and calm.*

*O love, O lovest, once thyself*
*    hath tasted of the peaceful blitheful calm,*
*        thou hath no further quest to make,*
*            no longer path, no further*
*                journey,*
*But standeth thee and draw and pine and low*
*    and bleat, but for thy calm,*

*And O love, how thee question,*
*    how reflect unto the pathway back,*
*And how thee plead and how thee sorrow,*
*    and still O love, how thee know,*
*        (Intellectually, which does not count)*
*How thy desire, thy non-relenting passionate*
*    ardent longing desire draweth this,*
*The yearned and longed for back, (as salt doth draw)*
*    within your arms, our arms, within our embrace.*

*So O love, standstill in thine desire deep-seated,*
*    rest within assured to once again,*
*Our Love, your Love, the peaceful blitheful calm*
*    shall reach out a hand for us,*
*Clasp tightly, wooing us, loving us,*
*    (as in the in-instant flash)*
*And shall not let, this time,*
*    let a-go.*
*        2/11/1998 TFE*


## The Tiny One Affords to the Infinite

*As if the universal Oneness,*
*    had unfolded to your perception,*
*Only to withdraw and align unto Itself again,*
*    —drawing you, in part only—*

## A Tiny But Radiant Light

*Still only for the time-being, the being in time,*
*    the becoming in time, unto that day,*
*The tiny one, the finite, affords to,*
*    Wholeheartedly, the massive One,*
*The whole, entirely, full-heart-feltly,*
*    unitedly, in and to the One.*

*O Powerful Source,*
*    Let it Be.*
*        9/11/2005*

## CHAPTER VI
## Endnote

Endnote 1

The Love, and ultimately the Joy, continue to slowly diminish. Yet, paradoxically, the joy continues to also silently flourish: this is not the flaming Joy as otherwise propounded herein, but a subtle contentedness and inward Joy.

As an aside, the severe declination of the Love Eternal was beginning to be decidedly apparent, and accounts for the basic structure of the second book, *The Greening Springing*. Meg Weeps for the Prophet and Sobs for the Eternal Love—Love Eternal.

# CHAPTER VII

## HEART-SOBBING DETRIMENTAL DECLINE—
## Ariseth Soul and Mind to God

### —With Thee the Vacant Intent Alone

*Veneration the Second—An Impermanent Selfishness*

The brief period of the detrimental decline with the loss of the Love Eternal engenders a mounting loathsome longing, a lonesomeness: thence arises a corresponding heightened emotion, a yearning plea. This state is wholly characterized by an artificial or false form of veneration, more of a selfishness, *unbalanced* in nature. One begins to pray and plead in ever lengthy dissertations to desperately beg for acknowledgment and full reinstatement of the gifts. I call this selfish plea Veneration the Second.

Veneration the Second attempts to draw a blessing toward oneself to acquire an advantage rather than to bestow a praise or impart a gratefulness. It gradually builds and mildly overshadows the loving thoughts and genuine devotion and feels sorry solely for itself. This state portends to digressing into its old worn-out hope rather than standing staunch on its already acquired faith, which is the affirmative knowing belonging to Veneration the First.

Veneration the First, where first the soul and mind truly rise to God, is the only true vacant intent alone. It flows freely and generously *outward* toward its sacred love in gratefulness and adoration. It yields and gives, "I wept in praise, and in glory, and thankfulness, in impassioned veneration…" Veneration the First thrives in a mellow tone. Veneration the Second takes little part with the legitimate first born.

This second veneration knows better than to be selfish, but it slips; it is temporary and wayward. It questions, but understands. Eventually during the decline of the gifts, the exaggerated emotion of Veneration the Second wears itself out, gives up, becomes non-vigilant and to all appearances, becomes nonexistent. The poetry best expresses the period of the detrimental decline: It is maudlin, yet sincere.

Poetry—Forth-Arising Prayers

Ebbs, Swells, Leaves it High-Water Mark, then Flows

*O Heavenly, Thou makest my heart yawn,*
    *open, gaping, craven, crying, yearning,*
        *languishing within your love,*
            *—the memory of your love,*
                *—your now, nearly*
                    *missing love.*

*O, O Heavenly if Thy desire draws,*
    *if longing-yearning-languishing-listless*
        *draws—the reverse of radiate—then so,*
*O Heavenly, Thy love grows, builds and nourishes*
    *Interior the faithful, loving, joyful, child,*
        *invisible to the naked, blatant, eye,*
            *yet felt, perceived, sincere.*

*O Heavenly tell me please, alert unto me to know,*
    *how does the both, the love instilled, the joyfulness,*
        *live beside the languishing-linger? live aside*
            *its opposite as day and night apart?*
                *(each to the other not to discern)*
                    *yet me perceiving*
                        *—living both?*

## A Tiny But Radiant Light

*Postscript:*
*And O, O Heavenly, though I speak of your missing love,*
*   —your love as missing, you and I we both know,*
*     your love is never truly ever missing,*
*       but ebbs sometimes, swells,*
*         leaves its high-water mark,*
*          then flows.*
*            5/3/1998 TFE*


## The Holier Defeated My Defeat

*Humanity, momentarily, got a hold of me,*
*And yanked me down so severely back to earth,*
*I lie and wallow, in seemingly, in self-defeat,*
*While all the while, while all the while, divinity,*
*Was gaining, again, the upper, firmer, holier hold*
*—The holier hand enraptured and defeated my defeat.*
*   1/20/1996 TGS*


## Truth Sustaining Truth

*O Spirit of Affinity, do not listen to me sob,*
*   and cry and carry on for your absence,*
*You know the blessing blessed is beyond profound,*
*   far beyond the wildest of finite's imagination,*
*Yet true all true and love all love with truth sustaining*
*   upholding truth, incredible, unbelievable,*
*      unimaginable, unsurmountable,*
*         undeniable, truth.*
*          5/26/1996 TGS*


## Meant of Creation—Life, Itself, A-Pulsing
## The Blossom

    The term the *Meant of Creation* is my concept of the mind's cognizance of one's true identify; of one's intimate relationship with the Eternal; it reaffirms the kindling which has occurred within the physical; the conjunction; the finite with the infinite.

The *central core* constitutes the tiny physical area wherein the enkindling bursts, the blossom. Thence flares the upward mobility, the *Nobility*, as if one were one with it. One is it. It is not seen, but *felt*, then outward and downward the influx and uniting proceed. Inborn with the kindling is, shed as a ray, a knowledge, an unshakable unfathomable faith: an Eternal life.

Selection from *Go as a Wisp Withon the Wind A-floating*

> *"Thou art thyself 'Creation,' the Life buoys up in thee,*
> > *has espied the sun, the wondersome, the guiding light,*
> *The bright, the solemnity, the 'future hope' a-currently,*
> > *and thee thyself, unknown just now unto thyself,*
> *Is basking in Life's presence—in the present—interiorly*
> > *—is reveling in its presence—as told to thee."*

Selection from *Go as a Wisp Withon the Wind A-floating*

> *"Thou art thyself*
> *The meant of creation, the Love abiding thee,*
> > *all tranquil calm Love's course withon,*
> *With every wisp, the wind, or hint of breeze,*
> > *Love's life applauding thee, a-lauding thee,*
> *And you O mild, now kindred, soul in thy recreation*
> > *—thy re-creation shall abide with Love,*

> *"With Love, the tranquil sea, the pond, the lake sedate,*
> > *a leisurely, broadcasting Love out and about*
> *For others soon to lavish upon. Now go and await*
> > *the presence more, in thy non-complaining,*
> *In thy leisure time, thy waning time a-waning,*
> > *thy cherished time abiding,*

> *"Love shall share with thee as thee let it,*
> > *and as thee share with others lavishly,*

## A Tiny But Radiant Light

*Love shall love thee liberally, generously.*
  *Go as a wisp withon the wind a-floating."*
    *3/10-4/23/1996 TGS*

## Poetry—Happy Hope to Substantial Faith

### Once the Blossom Bursts

*Feeling lost and all alone,*
  *no place right now to call my home,*
*Once having struck, been struck, by the flight of Right,*
  *the destiny called "Good,"*
*The purely earthly, pure mundane,*
  *relents itself, tugs back, harks back, pulls back,*
*And mourns and waits-waits-forth unto the morning "Sun."*

*And waits unto, and prays unto, its companion,*
  *its new-birth, the fountain spring, the lightning flash,*
*The joy, the laugh, the bubbling mirth, the Love itself,*
  *swelling, welling, burgeoning, flowering, arraying-forth,*
*—Displaying the Unknown known—the Known unto the unknown,*
  *known, to return.*

*For all the earth, the beauty, the sun, and moon and stars,*
  *the heavenly earthly vegetation, animals, birds, reptiles,*
*The swimming fish and all other manner of the material-corporal,*
  *—And our humanity, is plenteous and beauteous by far,*
*And strains our eyes and hearts in awe—its past its history,*
  *the future too, the purpose, the life, the "What is life?"*
*The "What is thought?" and its oft-times contrariety, the emotion,*
  *the logical and feeling, the Time and its space, dimension,*

*Challenge, hindrance, movement, flight, family, friends,*
  *acquaintances—men of wisdom, women of wisdom*
*Of encouragement, of inspiration. What is this?*
  *What of all of this stands up-to, within the reach,*
*Meets eye to eye, with absolute blossoming, furbishing,*
  *magnanimous, unutterable, truth,*

## Margaret Mary Stender

*—After once it espies, humanity espies,*
  *once the blossom bursts?*

The *"All the earthly tides and tidbits,"*
  *and youth, maturity, and age,*
Takes the seat, back-seat (even) unto the earthly joys and woes,
  the challenges, the daily work, activity, and thence all-else,
And though it works and plays, adheres to "its" responsibilities,
  it nary once forgets, or relents, it never once releases
Nor relinquishes its hold unto, its faith unto, its joy unto,
  its blossom, once blossomed, living now
Mercifully in the memory and radiating forth,
  hence forth.
      *7/27/1999 TFE*

## It is Time

O, O love of mine, please help me true,
  to find to feel the love of you.
"Eons" have trespassed since your appearance,
  the full accompaniment the wings,

The swishing rustle, the sounds,
  O beauteous the sounds,
The flights of wings a flapping,
  and then the strike,
The lightning strike,
  the unexpected,

The love of Love itself, the juncture
  in the middle center bursting,
Thence traveling down unto the arms,
  throughout the arms and hands
Then down the chest just below the arms
  and stopped, just stopped.

O, O love of me, so stopped
  and stayed then left,

## A Tiny But Radiant Light

*Nary to reach the pinnacle again,*
    *so hardship, O lot of me.*

*You left with me the gifts*
    *the quiet solemn peaceful calm,*
*Then the joyous laughter forming,*
    *the happiness beyond compare,*
*The knowledge of minds now left and gone,*
    *the lonesome knowing yearning mystery.*

*And me, O me, doing what I know to do,*
    *and all to no avail.*
*It's you, O generosity, the wings*
    *delivering, who holds the choice,*
*The decision, to visit to love,*
    *to ever come again,*
*Withhold your love or no.*
    *It seems I have no choice.*

*It has been, O love of mine,*
    *Eons quadrupled,*
*This July twenty-four. It is time!*
    *time again to alert the wings,*
*To bring, to usher in, to herald,*
    *your love sublime,*

*To take my equilibrium,*
    *to take my love in tow,*
*To never let me go, it is time,*
    *O heartfelt wondrous cheer,*
*O love beyond conception,*
    *it is time.*
        *5/25/1996 TGS*

*All Flaws Abolished by the Light*—A Vision, and *Three Landscape Paintings*—A Vision, appear in the Appendix.

Margaret Mary Stender

Port of Your Return—Love Doth Seethe and Whisper

*Port of Your* Return, the period principally offers a plethora of prophetic visions ordained to augment the inborn comprehension of eternal life; portends to one's destined Eternal *Beyond*; the visions are the bestowal of a *helping hand* and guidance.

With the implicit knowledge of one's inherent destiny, with eternal life assured, the visions tend to encourage one to be patient. Veneration the First again arises in a gentle unassuming nonchalant and comfortable mellow manner, which becomes a non-conscious priority: one lives it; stands-staunch in faith as if one were entranced, kneeling at the altar, facing upward with eyes wide open.

Poetry in View of the Happy Hope

Alert Withon the Top
—A Vision

Immortality

*A while back, some weeks or more,*
*Appeared within the view a scene,*
*A scene before my very eyes, and still a scene with me in view.*
*As from the top I peered withon the scene withof the two,*
    *Withof the me and withof one other, (Endnote 1)*
*Withon, withdown, the hill to speed-a-charging-forth full-tilt.*

*And as I watched the scene, the view withof the two,*
*—A me and another—right by my right by my side,*
*We charged and sped downhill, the me withon*
*The speeding trek withof, withby, another,*

*And—also—the me withon the top, atop, the hill!*

*And as I peered, withon within the scene appeared,*
*A-red, a light, withfar a-front ahead, and the thoughts*
    *—from the top,*

## A Tiny But Radiant Light

*"Will they make it? Will they make it? Will the red light*
    *—the stop—turn to green?"*

For from the vantage point, withof the top,
The knowledge that they could not slow or stop,
And the only vantage, advantage, they would have—is if
The red light would timely change to green and halt and stop,
    —the traffic oncoming from the other direction.

But so to wonder from the largest of long times—it appeared,
They speeding, unable in their advance to withstop
    —and me in thoughts of fear for their well-being.

Then suddenly, yet suddenly, the direction-the traveled
    —as if it met, they met, a tine, a V, (Endnote 2) in time,
Veered sharply toward the left onward, withon withtoward,
    —in the distance, the structures, some buildings,
And now sure, now certain to crash,

And at the speed, them, the me and one other,
Surely unable to survive, the pending crash, the hit,
The jolt withon the surface, withon the face,
Withof the buildings onward onto their left.

As me a-watching knowing far, afar in advance,
That they were certain to crash, and watching,
And watching, and peering and knowing
    —of the certain death.

Then as they approached, came very much near,
Onward unto the building to appear, they came,
And to my astonishment, much to my surprise,
They entered a door and disappeared from view.

Yet knowingly, yet knowingly, they certainly, would certainly,
Could certainly not stop, knew they were, their, our earthly lives,
    ended.

And as withon the scene, withon the watch—I watched knowingly.
Then the pulse withfrom the scene quenching waved,
    —abounded—bounded forth—withfrom withto me,

### Margaret Mary Stender

*And me I knew, the two within the scene, had ended*
  *—within the pulse, within the reverberation,*
    *—the pulsation, from the scene.*

*Yet me, the other me, the one withwatching withon the scene,*
*Withfrom the top—merely barely felt—but knew withof the stop*
*Withof the other, the earthly other, and me withfrom the top*
*Observed, and still remained, alerted—alert withon the top.*
*(Endnote 3)*
  *10/19/1997 TFE*


### Opened by An Unseen Hand
### —A Vision

*Reading Brother Lawrence:*
*A vision of a window,*
  *—Stuck,*
    *—Unstuck—Struck,*
*Opened by an unseen hand.*
  *11/15/1998 TFE*


### Never the Flame to Darken Out
### —A Vision

*The heart is warm and shining,*
  *ever doth it glow,*
*For Thou, the gift instilled,*
  *blazon in the soul.*

*Last week or so an item,*
  *interesting on TV.*
*It showed a window, closed,*
  *with candle before a-lit,*

*Then out! the candle goes,*
  *...and disappears.*

## A Tiny But Radiant Light

*Yet! within the vision*
*        of one involved,*
*The candle reappeared relit*
*        on the outer side.*

*Hearkening to hear, enlightening to see,*
*        enthralling to know and understand.*
*Yet, unsought, within another vision,*
*        freely given, a week or so thereafter,*
*Appeared within one's view, a fraction of moment,*
*        not even two,*
*A window stuck, long-stuck,*
*        as if from paint long-hardened,*
*Then unstuck, the "paint" gave loose,*
*        the window sprang open.*

*To the wondering mind*
* Never to query, to question, or doubt,*
*        the window hath sprung open,*
*Nary the candle to diminish. Never,*
*        the flame to darken out.*
*        11/16/1998 TFE*

Currently and curiously, in April 2009, while prodding through what I call the technical last half of this work, an exceptional event occurred. In astonishment a question arose; is the forthgoing two poems a mere coincidence, or, in fact, could it represent the *Unseen Hand,* of a long lost memory which never came to mind until now, as penned in the paragraph below?

On April 21, 2009, today, I reiterate a brief portion of history: I see another truth. Last week, with the intention of giving my granddaughter, Nickole, a sorted and packed box of books for her home, my eyes happened upon the very top book. Apparently, while packing the box, the recognition of a certain special book went unnoticed.

Yet now, with the books sitting next to the chair by my side and with Nickole and her friend sitting across the room, I glanced downward. Astonished! I grabbed the book and blurted out, "I know this man." With meager thought afore hand, with a fragmented form of subconscious memory, my immediate second thought was, "If I know this man, then the book must be autographed." In a rush and dither, I opened the front cover and to my sheer surprise, it *was* in fact autographed!

Yogi Raushan Nath had written, "For Peggy Giem, with all the good wishes and kindest regards, Raushan Nath, 11/8/71." (Even then in 1971, and before then, as you know, I was searching.) Now, I was barely able to lay *The Unseen Hand* aside, (Endnote 4) to continue the conversation with my guests. My mind strained elsewhere while striving to be courteous. The book's sudden reappearance and recovery flashed forth a long silent memory of a *formative* vision, now suddenly vibrant in its detail; a memory which I had stowed away, which had become a part of my being, but for which I had neglected over the intervening years.

One night in my perennial search, I was invited, or more likely, found out by *chance* about a small gathering to be held in a private home. Perhaps, I invited myself along with another person of whose name I do not recall. Or, perhaps, that other person invited me. Again, I do not recall. Yogi Raushan Nath's friends in Kalamazoo, Michigan, had invited merely a few persons over to their home to meet their out-of-town guest and his wife, to hear him speak and to learn to meditate. I, somehow, was fortunate to be among them.

Herein, is the other truth: We sat on the floor in committed meditation chanting "Om." I recall that I was leaning against a wall. The OM was foreign to me; the concentration was not. Therein, I experienced what I now recall as my first vision, nevertheless forgotten until now.

In an instance and for an instant, in today's language, I perceived myself as being pure intelligence; pure thought, with the added incongruent perception of possessing a collar, similar to a clown's huge wide buoyant collar, below the chin and around the neckline. All conscious perception of what existed, or perhaps was nonexistent, below this collar was eliminated from perception, from my *person*. No thought of the material world entered in.

## A Tiny But Radiant Light

I existed only from the top of the neck upward. In my incredulity, shortly thereafter, I related the vision to Yogi Raushan. I do not recall his exact reply, it was a relatively nondescript positive and, although of greater length, was similar to "You are a very intuitive person."

In any event, it was complimentary and I was surprised and pleased. I left the home feeling elated and genuinely fortunate to have been among them. (Endnote 5)

# CHAPTER VII
# Endnotes

Endnote 1
I am both the Observer peering from the top and the Observed, with one other by my side, on the harrowing downward ride.
In the vision, the "they" included this writer (and another unknown). This is one of the genuinely rare instances of being both the observer and the participant, the observed.

Endnote 2
The shortest expanse of time; in the twinkling of an eye; the endpoint of a decision, where one veers off in one direction or another.

Endnote 3
The earthly life ended, and the Life was preserved withon the top.

Endnote 4
THE UNSEEN HAND, A handbook of yoga way of life for self-realization, YOGA RAUSHAN NATH, Forward by DR. KARAN SINGH, RAJIV PUBLICATIONS, NEW DELHI, June 1971. Distributors: Trimuri Publications, W-152, Greater Kailash-I, New Delhi-48. PRINTED IN INDIA BY: NEW INDIA PRESS, K-BLOCK, CONNAUGHT CIRCUS, NEW DELHI-1.

Endnote 5
Ibid., THE EIGHTFOLD PATH OF YOGA, THE SADHANA, p 105. Yogi Raushan Nath teaches the proper state of mind, prior to the chant, OM. Essentially, "...recite, Om !Om !gradually lower your voice to a whisper..." until you reach Samadhi, which "in the beginning is a state of the still mind... "( You do lose the sense of time and space for quite some time while lost in a state of Samadhi.)" I encourage each person to secure and read the wisdom of Yogi Raushan Nath.

## CHAPTER VIII

## FINAL WORDS—Rest in the Knowledge

Please bear with me for a slight summary and a few extracurricular comments: The July 1991 mystical experience with its faculties and multi-facets and their range of influence, passivity and passion, pacified or raged in the heart and mind instilling their influence and momentum.

\*\*\*

The enkindling with its flaming upward above the head awakened, embrightened and embraced the entire being with its rapture and knowledge. The immediate emanating calm and love breathed forth the individual and combined, immediate or evolving effects along with the accompanying enhanced emotions. The fervent first veneration—genuine adoration—for the Eternal blossomed into an unchallenged heartfelt love for mankind.

After one week befell the initial colossal loss of the perpetual calm, then a second reduction after three plus months dealt a rigorous blow. The gifts remaining after the second declination nevertheless remained sufficient to calm, to majestically inspire; three years later to engender and write the poetry and to generate the preponderance of energy necessary to focus primarily on the poetry and secondarily to maintain an occupation, a home, and a family. The differing degrees of the various combinations of the gifts intermingled, crested and waned, for roughly five to six years.

Thence ensued another noticeable, albeit gradual tapering off of all the gifts nearly all together: the Love and to a minor degree the relative newcomer, the jubilant Joy. The mystical Calm, the especial priceless jewel, with the indwelling presence, lived noticeably for an extended period.

Nevertheless, the underpinning miraculous jubilant joy though waning and its loyal sidekick, Youth, steadily thrived, remained steadfast and true much longer. The two compatriots, the two joys, counterbalanced the obvious decline.

Youth, *being young*, seems to live heartily in the *outer atmosphere*. Eventually, though, even the joy and youth mellowed or merged and cohered into what appears to be a permanent serene gladness, or happiness, an oneness, a unified content. The exception is that one feels deeply the pangs of another.

The knowledge acquired of the evening, especially the moment with its majestic offspring, never left nor diminished, rather ensconced in the deep recesses of the mind; embedded it flourished. The knowledge, a knowing of the infinite unity, also entwined itself in the conscious mind relentless, still to this day is determined to speak. Knowledge and its instigation support a person in their natural life, and influence in every aspect; prods one to further search; loves one; encourages one; chides one; weeps with one; keeps one in-line; adheres to the consciousness every waking hour.

The poetry began at the three-year mark. By now, 2008, should I desire to write poetry, it is only possible by first relocating the interior rhythm. The buoyant joy and the inspiration have generally left. The content, the reason for the initial poetic format, has principally been expressed and expressed true to its nature.

The only current, yet unequivocal, imposing or compelling-prompting is to set forth the mystical experience in its undivided merit, in clarity; in its entirety in one cohesive whole. Still, the precise mode of ignition—the enkindling—hinted at, is left to the reader to discover for himself or herself: The reader's experience, once initiated, will be far more beneficial, wholly-full-fledged, if there is no expectation laid out in advance (Remember the severe detriment of the annihilating thought?). The enkindling is beyond laudable and is worth the lifetime to secure.

Perhaps it is relevant to further emphasis just how critical the primary gifts were to the writing of the poetry. I was working an extraordinary number of hours as community development director for the City of Kalamazoo. There was no extra time, no extra energy. However, during the period of the writing, there was sufficient time and, astonishingly, there was prolific energy, energy in abundance. I was able to get up at 3:30 or 4:00 a.m., go to bed late and work diligently on the weekends with the poetry. I seldom tired. The energy held firm.

After *eighteen months* and the completion of the two books, I did begin to feel a deep fatigue as the declination of the gifts—all of the gifts in their wax and wane—began to affect the body and infect the mind with a dreadful fulsome sorrow strictly due to the inclining loss. During this period, *The Forever Entwined* and *Wonderment* emerged. This work primarily encompassed the entire period of the full-blown detrimental decline and a soul-searching lamentation.

(The loss manifested itself in a manner mildly akin to what the young Pablo Picasso must have felt during his blue period; the period following the unnecessary death of his young friend. Picasso painted only in tones of mournful blue.) Although, I wrote in lamentation, still, the lamentation was in measure modified by the Joy: and, I always knew that the loss was not permanent. Those assets remain silent, though ensconced within. This appears to be a contradiction, yet, it is not, and it is beyond my ability to unravel or to effectively explain it.

Visions began, prior to the poetry, as noted in *Megan's Story* and emerged in their full veracity during the period of the declination, though, currently, visions seldom appear unless there is to be a distinct fracture of life's pathway ahead. A vision will warn of *something to occur*, and in a vague manner will divulge the general outcome and time frame, short or long. It is unlikely, but it may inform one of the "who" will be involved or affected, but it will not disclose the detailed nature of the event itself.

In essence, the evening and moment spun my life on a 180-degree pivot and preserved it there. The decision to "set the gift aside to complete a temporary laborious task at the office" at the three-month mark, was the most irresponsible incomprehensible decision of my entire life. At the time, I believed the Calm would return. It has never returned in total; not the intensity, not the inspiration, not *anything* in the same manner, and I have lived to regret this decision a myriad times over.

Once the prelude, and the state of illumination, is experienced, in the earthly or natural life, there is no forgetting, no ignoring, no living totally outside the sway of its lush greenery, its prompting, and its unending and unyielding virtuous nature and influence. And, there is no desire to! It completes one. And though certain effects dwindle, its radiance dwells in the consciousness, flares outward in love, inhabits and augments the being, and "both" live conjointly as one.

This slight review is repetitious. Nonetheless, all poems were reread this month for content and for their date of creation, in an attempt to assure that no error exists in this narrative. Although the gifts themselves are thoroughly and ardently known—impregnated in the mind and heart, deep within the being—and need no review. As previously stated, thinking in retrospect, the precise period of their separate activity is not as clear. However, the chronology is essentially accurate. The review was prudent and productive.

One may believe that the mystical experience was of little pivotal account since so little is able to be reported, and since the only consideration herein concerns the events of the evening to morning of one miraculous night and the consequent out-birthing of its resultant faculties—which I frequently call, gifts—though, it is serenely monumental! It is only that I am unable to effectively speak to the height and breadth of the mystical experience, or to the light of understanding that soars into one's life.

It is my hope that the poetry, with all its inherent emotionalism streaming and beaming, will speak competently to the Moment's essential bestowal and to the light of understanding that it grants.

# A Tiny But Radiant Light

Moreover, the Moment, the Enkindling, grants an understanding to the writings, metaphor, or hidden message of other persons.

The poetry alludes to the life of the unity living and thriving in the finite world, bearing the finite into the infinite, and the infinite into the finite. It is clear that the infinite, the eternal, runs concurrently as an *underpinning*; as sun-lit glistening bedrock is to the prolific radiant stream.

The decline of the gifts is the logical succession in all outward nature. Even though, one may not *wish* a diminishment with its accompanying lamentation, it comprises the necessary counterpart to the sacred highlight with its joy; the *centripetal* to the *centrifugal*, the ebb and tide, the light and the dark; the wave with its ebb and flow, the ultimate equivalence (with the rebirth of its crest). The thunderous pulsing winds—with the enkindling of embrightenment—emerged through the darkness. This writer rests in the serene knowledge of eternal life.

END Part I

Margaret Mary Stender

# CHAPTER IX

# LET US TAKE A SLIGHT FORK IN THE ROAD
Affinity

### A Trudge Along Another Path
### Proceed at an Unknown Pace

The 1991 experience was dynamic and instantaneous, and certain knowledge of its spiritual origin, nature, and distinction were born concurrently. I knew of no specific name for it (this sounds naive, yet is true), and for many years I spoke of it to no one.

In December1998, after the completion of the majority of the poems, including those in the first two books and the majority of those in the third, after the *fact*, I discovered the *Wheaton College, Christian Classics Ethereal Library* on the Internet. In perusing the titles of the books, I inadvertently came upon Richard Rolle's *Fire of Love*. The words leaped out at me.

With a jolt—a colossal thunderbolt—of recognition, as in a lightning flash, I comprehended the significance of the title *Fire of Love*! The flame, the glowing radiant of love, also resided with me. It spoke of itself in the poetry. Thereafter, I read the works of numerous Mystics (a new term in my naive life) and now most importantly, I had a name for the experience. I had had a *Mystical* experience.

Richard Rolle and John Yepes vindicated my work, not that I ever believed that the work needed vindication; I knew better. It is reasonably certain that Richard Rolle was among the first of the mystics whose works I ever read. However, at some distinction in my early life, I read the *Cloud of Unknowing* and undoubtedly read St. Frances without realizing they were mystics, or at least to today's mind the term mystic did not register.

As you know, I was also familiar with those well-known persons written about by Bucke in his book *Cosmic Consciousness,* and certainly knew of the term and somewhat of the manner of the illumination experience.

The point in reiterating the history above is to freely and joyously acknowledge the time-serving influence that people of history have had by virtue of their person, as well as through their writings. Without their sound footing to build upon, and especially without a genuine faith and trust, I believe that at-least-I would be completely *mired in the mud.*

A critical related point, is that it appears that the ancient mystics wrote for the sole purpose of sharing their experience to the benefit of searching others; in other words, the mystics wrote long before the primary objective of writing was in large part for fame or for dollars and, therefore, undoubtedly can be relied on indiscriminately.

They were frequently urged by others of their ilk to write of their spiritual journey, their sweeping knowledge and their undeniable understanding of spiritual life. As a result of their experience, their various spiritual qualities, the illumination showed in their face and in their demeanor, in their actions, and in their written correspondence.

This current writer, I, dare not even tread in the age-old dust of the footprints of the great mystics or of the men and women described by Bucke: Still there was something special...and enduring.

## CHAPTER X

## RICHARD MAURICE BUCKE, M.D.—The Marks of Cosmic Sense

This section relies heavily on the writing and authority of Richard Maurice Bucke, M.D., set forth in *Cosmic Consciousness*. Bucke conducted a prolonged *Study in the Evolution of the Human Mind* and elaborated upon his lifelong work, research, findings, and the evidence of those findings, together with his convictions and theories. The subtitle on the front cover of a subsequent edition reads,"A classic investigation of the development of man's mystic relation to the infinite." (Endnotes 1, 2)

In the *Man and the Book*, the Introduction by George Moreby Acklom describes Richard Maurice Bucke, the Canadian doctor, (Endnote 3) as "anything but an ordinary professional man. He was a matter-of-fact scientist...a man of highly developed imaginative faculty and endowed with an enormous memory...In 1876 he was appointed Superintendent of the newly built Provincial Asylum for the insane at Hamilton, Ontario... In 1882 he became Professor of Mental and Nervous Diseases at Western University (London, Ontario). In 1888 he was elected President of the Psychological Section of the British Medical Association, and in 1890 President of the American Medico-Psychological Association."

Acklom goes on to assert there was another side of him of greater lasting importance. He explains that in 1867 Bucke received a visitor who "quoted some verses of Walt Whitman's to him" and that "their effect on him was extraordinary, instantaneous and permanent."

## A Tiny But Radiant Light

"In the spring of 1872..." Bucke, while on a visit to England, experienced Illumination. Acklom details Bucke's experience as quoted from the *Proceedings and Transactions of the Royal Society of Canada*. (Endnote 4) Essentially, Bucke spent the evening with friends reading the poetry of well-known poets, including Walt Whitman. On his way home, "all at once without warning...he found himself wrapped around...by a flame-colored cloud...he knew the light was in himself...there came upon him a sense of exultation, of immense joyousness..." Thereupon, "...an intellectual illumination quite impossible to describe...leaving thenceforward for always an aftertaste of Heaven."

*Cosmic Consciousness*, Part I, *First Words*, also written by Acklom, generally repeats the delineation of the evening of Bucke's illumination in essentially the identical words. However, it continues with Bucke "...knew that the Cosmos is not dead matter but a living Presence, that the soul of man is immortal...all things work together for the good...the foundation principle of the world is what we call love..." (Endnote 5)

The chapter on John Yepes, St. John of the Cross, Bucke references Yepes by saying, "Yepes' thought is, "The soul that knows that God is in it is blessed, but the soul in which God wakes is that which is supremely blessed." (Endnote 6)

Based upon Bucke's knowledge and insight revealed in *Cosmic Consciousness*; his incredible personal illumination experience which set him firmly upon an avowed path; the incredible massive quantity of research delineated in his book emphasizing the numerous correspondence with other individuals which he recognized as those persons having achieved cosmic consciousness; upon Bucke's lasting friendship with Whitman; and the virtue gained from his lifelong love of poetry and reading, it is abundantly clear that he was uniquely qualified to profess the faculty of cosmic consciousness.

It is as if this personal illumination along with its message and advantage, and the especial authorship of *Cosmic Consciousness*, was his chosen and dedicated life's destiny.

\*\*\*

Richard Maurice Bucke, the Canadian doctor, identified several faculties which are immediately gained as a result of undergoing the experience of illumination, and of which results in the corresponding acquisition of the faculty of cosmic consciousness; the faculty, the attributes—gifts—he called the marks of cosmic sense. Let us turn directly to these marks.

The marks of the cosmic sense (Endnote 7) existing prior to, during, or post illumination are: a subjective light; a moral elevation; an intellectual illumination; the acquired sense of immortality; the loss of the fear of death; the loss of the sense of sin; the suddenness, instantaneousness, of the awakening; the previous character of the man, intellectual, moral, and physical; the age of illumination; a charm added to the personality so that men and women are generally strongly attracted to the person; and there is a transformation of the subject as seen by others when the cosmic sense is actually present.

Bucke further explains that when one passes from simple to self-consciousness, and when one passes from self-consciousness to cosmic consciousness, there are derived two chief elements. These, he concluded, are "added consciousness ...which instructs without any new experience or process of learning" and "added faculty..." where "he takes on enormously greater capacity both for learning and initiating." (Endnote 8)

Bucke distinguished thirteen persons as complete cases of cosmic consciousness, or in other words of persons who are in possession of the cosmic sense. Among those named are men of stature, Walt Whitman, Plotinus, Dante Alighieri, Jacob Behmen, Honorè de Balzac and several others. Each person is recognized to be of great spiritual orientation; each is well-known in our history. Bucke further identified numerous persons whom he believed to be lesser, imperfect and doubtful instances. He frequently spoke of imperfect cases as being in the twilight of cosmic consciousness.

Justin Kaplin says of Bucke, "He had found that ecstatic illuminations were by no means so uncommon as supposed— ordinary people leading ordinary lives testified to them as well as great moral and ethical leaders, a conclusion supported by subsequent researchers..." (Endnote 9)

Bucke posits that during the onset of illumination, many a man or woman, being in a passive mood initially, became aware or were surprised or astounded by seeing internally what appeared to be flame, a vibrant bright light, or of being immersed or enveloped in a pink cloud, (This is the selfsame knowledge which leaped with cold-brazen-feet, stomping into the mind of this writer, in the vesture of one devastating annihilating thought, mentioned earlier in *Thunderous Sound*.) waylaying the night or day, surrounding him or her. This he identified as a first manifestation in the process of illumination.

\*\*\*

The recounting of my personal revelation, an awakening in the twentieth century, is a tiptoeing in the twilight; nonetheless, the revelation is monumental, and for its informative value should not be completely overlooked.

The purpose of the next few pages is to delineate Bucke's eleven marks of the cosmic sense and, thereafter, correlate the various aspects of the mystical experience of the evening and moment with each of those independent marks. The comparison whether it corroborates, or more importantly whether it is significantly divergent in its nature, is meant to augment and to clarify information contained in the first part of this current work.

Further, and more essentially, the purpose of the comparison is to effectively determine the depth, or the strength, of the enkindling with its embrightenment and flare in an effort to discern the level to which each element measures up, or especially how far it falls short of meeting-the-*mark*—forgive the play on words.

Let us now turn directly to Bucke's marks of the cosmic sense. Listed first is the individual mark, which is followed by a significantly abbreviated (Endnote 10) form of Bucke's definition. The correspondent element of the evening's embrightenment experience, comment or clarification appears second.


**Subjective Light: ...has a sense of being immersed in a flame, rose-colored cloud, or perhaps rather a sense that the mind is itself filled with such a cloud of haze. (Endnote 11)**

In the instance of the evening, the moments preceding the enkindling, there is a strict divergence. There was no perception of any form of light, no flame, no color. The mind was not filled with a haze nor in any manner does this personal instance precisely resemble the first of Bucke's marks of the cosmic sense. There are exquisite distinctions, however, which cause wonder to the earthly mind.

Writing on this date, November 7, 2007, in retrospect, I realize this *breaking through the darkness* has never been spoken of in the poetry. The sanctity of the bursting-forth of the enkindling always took precedence, always so overshadowed, that until now in addressing the "flame or rose-colored cloud" little thought has been given to the darkness which preceded, beyond and before, the thunderous swiftly rushing of winds. (Refer to Chapter III)

There was a clear visual distinction prior to the winds-a-rushing; precisely as the momentum broke through the darkness. Yet, no vision other than the darkness was truly present. There appeared an ultra-brief slightly transparent movement, or to today's mind, a quavering attending the onset of the raging winds.

This *image* is in some measure similar to the earthly perception of heat rising in the air, though, there was no "rise," but an impression of a sort opening outward horizontally as the winds virtually broke through with a gigantic thunderous force from what *appeared* to be a flat vertical plane, or wall, facing toward the perception and from a short distance; as if the activity were happening near the corner of the room (my bedroom) at a distance of eight to ten feet and slightly to the right, although it remained in the still-inner-darkness of the being.

## A Tiny But Radiant Light

(It appeared at a distance, yet was within.) The view was similar to a broad pencil being thrust swiftly with force through taut black paper held vertically. There was no pencil, of course, but thunderous winds; clearly apparent was the perception and knowledge that the winds broke through creating a "hole" in the vertical darkness. There was no view of the winds, but the thunderous rushing vibrating or rhythmic sounds. The winds caused the attendant rhythm.

The *distance* between the source of the perception and the invisible vertical plane, obstruction or *wall*, had depth (eight to ten feet) and was black, and the *plane* itself (the wall, itself, wherein the breaking forth in the darkness "actually" took place) was black. There was no depth beyond, as behind the vertical plane, where the winds *originated*. There was no true visual distinction, yet there was a clear perception. There was definitely a vertical obstructing aspect, still, all was darkness; still, with no light; visible yet non-visible in the ordinary sense. There was a distinguishing, but no light. No color.

This breaking-forth through the darkness startled and awakened the mind with a marked immediate perception of the thunderous winds. The breaking-forth was recorded in the alerted mind, yet there appeared to be no time elapse in the *no-time-elapse* between it and when the impact of the forthcoming swift winds struck the body: struck within the middle of the head with a bursting-forth, (Endnote 12) and with its flare of consciousness upward.

Instantly upon the winds' impact, there incurred a two-way split of its effect—a two-way transference—such as with a fork in the road. The mind in amazement followed the physical manifestation in stark wonderment, while the body felt the imposing effect of the vibratory strike, of the physical manifestation, of the bursting-forth, the enkindling; an astonishing intimate revelation!

The conferment of the vibration or pulsation, was derived as a result of the impact of the forceful vibratory sound of the winds. With the conferment to the physical body, the transfer, the winds were no more. (Endnote 13) The mind in awe and composed peaceful sheer-pure astonishment continued to *watch*, to assess, to tally of the wonder; the physical ecstasy; the union; the rapture conferred; as it traveled noticeably and wondrously, above the head (flared above the head), then near simultaneously to the upper body.

The second distinction, a preeminent revelation, is the concrete consciousness (the affirmed immediate awareness) of the bursting forth as it flared above the head conjoined with the consciousness, the knowledge, that this extended "region" is part of the personal being. This consciousness of being *in this newly defined region,* combined with the pulsating physical manifestation, lasted only for a moment. Yet the manifestation of the physical sensation in "what" one would normally consider to be "their normal physical body" lasted for several moments.

(Although, singular, the winds always appear as "winds," plural. The winds are "one," singular. Indeed, there were many raging loud blusterous, rhythmic—resounding in their force—winds: a chaos of winds. Never was there *a* wind. [As an aside, logically, which does not count in this instance, never could there have been *a* wind. One *wind* could not have been vibratory.] Although, in succeeding years, the winds always expressed, or appeared, to a less degree; they [in this case truly plural] expressed themselves to the perception as *wings* or as a flutter.

Generally, the sound was combined with a racing, or especially with a swiftly-rushing, aspect. [Visions too, oftentimes appeared with a rushing or racing aspect.]) But the true "formal" winds, the winds of the breaking-forth, never reappeared in its full contingent.

**Moral Elevation: ...he is...bathed in an emotion of joy, assurance, triumph, "salvation." ...the feeling, when fully developed, is not that a particular act of salvation is effected, but that no special salvation is needed...It is this ecstasy... with which the *poets*, as such, especially occupy themselves...**

## A Tiny But Radiant Light

There was never an initial sense of triumph in the traditional sense of the word, only awe. If the potential was ever viable, it would have been an ultra-mild sense of triumph, muted or completely blanketed by the thunderstruck recognition of the sovereign event.

Certainly triumph did not rise to the realm of the self-conscious mind. The consciousness was mellow, satiated, loving, kind, solemn, nearly sacred, reclining as to be completely overthrown, hidden in the cleft of the rock so to speak, reclining in the entrance, basking in the light of the noonday sun, lulled by the knowledge and the calm of the blazing eternal Sun, and the warmth of the celestial day.

A soft gentle joy settled in the aftermath of the enkindling, which was accompanied by a solemn gratefulness and, even more than a recognition, there was an immediate insight that an especial rare gift had been *given*; engifted.

Under no circumstance could this precise occurrence have actually been sought. To my adamant belief, under no circumstance could there have been a true sense of triumph, since no knowledge of the precise nature of the birth existed prior to the experience, and especially since the birth, the enkindling, instilled in the awareness the knowledge that this was a bestowal and sanctified.

The direct knowledge of the sudden enkindling, the surcharge, was evident; the divine had aligned with the human and flared upward, radiating a prolific profusion over approximately one fifth of the body. The word *ecstasy, a physical sensation heightened, far beyond any that otherwise belongs to the merely self-conscious life*—though recognized by the self-conscious life—perfectly describes the enkindling and its flare as it traveled with its sustained magnified sensation, with its immediate effect upon the physical body.

From this moment forward the individual is newborn, never to relent completely to the old barbarian and now abandoned ways and theories: all prior perspective dramatically changes. Never again, would one be *merely* human.

Margaret Mary Stender

Having forcefully stated there was never an initial sense of triumph, three years after the evening when the soul was buoyantly happy a poem was written which expressed a triumphal joy.

### The Soul Is Triumphant

*The Soul is triumphant,*
*It "worked its own way" out.*
*The joy it possesses,*
*Worth multi times what "it,"*
*"This world is all about."*

*Inherent joy has worked,*
*Itself, its own way through,*
*The drawing, the piercing*
*Angry discord and the*
*Earthly love upon the earth,*
*To reveal inwardness,*
*Liberty and set it free.*

*Inherent, love, has flamed*
*Into the outermost,*
*Within the earthly love,*
*A flame within a flame,*
*A light within a light,*
*To dwell upon this earth*
           *11/26/1994*

The emotion of joy was thoroughly addressed previously. However, "Immortality," or the recognition of being immortal is instilled, coagulated, (*coagulated*, an inordinate word, but apt) within the being, concurrent with the uniting in the enkindling.

### Life is Purely Life

*Life a self-fulfilling fact,*
*Sufficient evidence unto itself,*
*Sufficiently historically documented,*
*Life is in the present,*

## A Tiny But Radiant Light

*Is, was, and always, will be,*
*In the present, is the present.*
*"Life" is synonymous with "present."*
*Living "in" the present,*
*Is living, being present, in eternity.*
*Life by its very nature lives,*
*Life by its very nature,*
*By definition,*
*Cannot, will not, not exist,*
*Life is purely, starkly, life.*
*12/24/1994*

The awakening of the intellect did occur in that a sacred knowledge *within the hierarchy* was imparted in the most magnanimous manner. There is solely the mystical experience which blossomed with the aforesaid knowledge, which professed itself in an artistic manner, and which continues to birth forth its distinctive spiritual qualities; its continuing influence; and its ability to clear the path ahead: and, to the finite mind, the recognition of the diametrical 180-degree transition in life; the poetry and what is felt (what is gleaned in the reading—the rhythm instilled in the inspired verse) which trails in the undertone; the chronology of previously unknown attributes; and what is perceived in this current written work.

There was no "seeing into the root of all mysteries." There was the mere glimpse, which occurred after the evening and moment as presented in *Embodiment of Harmony,* (Endnote 14) with the observation of the heavenly bodies, orbs, planets, all moving in infinite silence, harmony, orbiting in accord. This vision is consequential; notwithstanding, it does not precisely meet Bucke's criteria.

**Sense of Immortality: …a sense of immortality… could better be compared to that certainty of distinct individuality, possessed by each one, which comes with and belongs to self-consciousness.**

Immediately with the enkindling, there was no longer a mere knowledge of, or a hope of, eternity, or immortality. *Faith* becomes tangible, unquestionable, undeniable, concrete; faith transforms into a knowing, becomes an essential part of the being, an endowment engifted—a *Knowledge Known*. One merely "Knows." One merely sings and broadcasts their heartfelt lightness and joy, yet knows not *how* they know of immortality.

*Sea unto Ourselves, Lull Too*, and a selection from *All the While* appear in the Appendix; the poems proclaim the immortality.


**Loss of the Fear of Death: …it simply vanishes.**

To appropriately locate the added gift "of the loss" of the fear of death and of the loss of the sense of sin, each engendered as a result of the illumination or embrightenment experience, it is important to acknowledge that the loss of the fear of death may be properly located in the section *Evening and Moment,* or it may be properly located in the section *New Life Living Within*. These two "losses" rank with the elite.

The instilled advantage is monumental in scope, yet subtle in nature. At a critical juncture, the mind becomes aware that *it* no longer fears death, and realizes that the fear seemingly disappeared at the moment of the mystical experience. In other words, the astonishment does not occur during the evening at the moment, but looms when one actually consciously recognizes that the dreadful fear is gone.

The advantage, the freedom from fear, is instilled concurrently with the knowledge of immortality and one lives and restructures their life accordingly. However, for a prolonged period, the person is absorbed in the more prominent physical experience and the overpowering explicit knowledge of immortality, and this "non-fear" only tiptoes into light, into recognition, somewhat later.

Life simply lives. There is no longer a question of whether there is a "death" in the traditional sense of the word death. All

## A Tiny But Radiant Light

further *entirety-of-life* is affirmatively addressed from the standpoint of immortality. The *knowledge of immortality* and the *loss of the fear of death* are as a right and left hand—as two sides of the same golden coin—the knowledge of immortality lives in the foreground in the light and the loss of the fear of death reclines as a helpmate within the shadow. The mind, the understanding, takes the shape of a foundation, rather than a structure; death has naught to fear.

Selection from *Let Us Think and Feel Together*

*It wrote of its first love, the love, Love Eternal, inborn in it,*
    *the bursting-forthing at one time in the mind, and traveling,*
*Thenceforth, forthwith, throughout the upper body.*
    *It loved, and imparted a joyous glow—an immediate*
    *—then later*
*A laughing flow, and it never thought to write, it loved*
    *and lingered throughout the day, throughout the night,*

*And this love, swept me, kept me right along with it and brought*
    *its gifts, presented to me, a knowingness of immortality,*
*A sincere and genuine love instilled, in-planted, within,*
    *and for three+ months it lived with me openly,*
*Calmfully, then it left, yet left its gifts.*
    *12/25/1996 TGS*

Selection from *Strengthen Our Path*

*The loss, a grateful loss, appearing sometime afterward,*
    *or recognition of, or its growing in me,*
*The loss of the fear of death, the release of worry, the long*
    *attached now non-attached—*
    *11/5/1995 TGS*


**Loss of the Sense of Sin: …It is not that the person escapes from sin; but he no longer sees that there is any sin in the world…**

The sense of sin simply vanishes in the manner identical to the annihilation of the fear of death: At some critical point, the mind suddenly becomes aware and wonders *aloud* whether there is no sin, or whether there is no conscience.

In passing, the poem below merely acknowledges the loss of the sense of sin in the most nonchalant and non-consequential manner, while, in reality, it is still questioning whether the conscience is no longer functioning, or whether there is no sin to enliven and en-swell the conscience. Perhaps, this mark of the cosmic sense is best responded to by offering the first two lines of the poem, *For the Absence of Its Lily*, which was written during the decline of certain of the particular gifts.

*After the dawn of day has struck,*
*is there no conscience or is there no sin?*

Eventually, the gift of "the loss of the sense of sin" dims. Its diminishment causes no lamentation; becalmed, one continues to maintain the path toward *right*. However, "the loss of the fear of death" never diminishes! It preserves its hierarchal status boldly starkly in the limelight.

Gained with succeeding years of experience, here are a few extra comments with respect to the incredible conscience: It appears that while under the exalted influence of the enlightenment, embrightenment, the established union with the Love Eternal renders the *normal* conscience temporarily mute.

The Love Eternal assumes full joint control with the conscious mind of the physical being—as if in joint-control. There exists an inherent true *recognition and knowing* of the right-of-way. The co-owner, the individual, is faithfully *guided* as if by a hidden light, or a silent sound, and *automatically* enforces their now enlightened or embrightened path. One largely considers of providing the advantage to others, to *making* "things right." (Endnote 15)

After writing the above paragraph in the greatest sincerity, I must acknowledge that approximately four years after the evening—the purport of this narrative—there was a whimsical

## A Tiny But Radiant Light

satire, a questioning of what appeared to the self-conscious mind to be a distinct contradiction to the purview of the "conscience." I wrote a poem titled *Goes Its Way a Cautioning* (Endnote 16) which poked fun and questioned its arduous, and what seemed to be needless, effort on *my* behalf; whether or not "conscience" was or is an apt term if "There is no sin."

As each person is aware, under normal circumstances there is definitely a steep *persuasion* to keep one on track or target, to keep the right, or the right-of-way. This concept was firmly in the mind in 1995 when *Macro Goal* was written. During that period, there was also no direct answer to this form of the questioning of oneself. The conscience seems to serve two purposes, to remedy, but primarily to avoid the necessity for remedy. The Conscience serves but one master.

For a time, one seems to affirmatively recognize there is no sin, yet works diligent-overtime to keep on the straight and narrow—to do "the right"; one lives it. The curious conscious mind does not always understand the apparent contradiction and spends amounts of time attempting to sort it out, all to no avail.

None-the-less, even under the influence of the embrightenment, humans, being human ["Being human" is questionable terminology, as it serves merely as a grand excuse] backslide slightly on occasion, although not severely, nor for a prolonged period; then, there is a swift severe vaulting-back to right, as if one's spring was coiled too tight and suddenly snapped into its rightful position.

Now. Why was so much time spent on elucidating "conscience?" Answer, simply because I, the conscious mind, I, do not understand it. Conscience is *there,* and Conscience is not there.


**Suddenness, Instantaneous, of the Awakening: can be compared with nothing so well as with a dazzling flash of lightning in a dark night...**

One cannot formulate the words to describe the immediacy with which the "two," the divine and the earthly, interact. It is as if the match struck the flint and burst into flame in the selfsame fraction of an instant, and united the two in flame.

In this instant the strike aligned with the suddenness of the thunderous rushing of winds breaking forth in the darkness and jarring the mind into acute alert recognition, then the no-time-lapse prior to the momentum—the winds striking and enkindling—bursting-forth the pulsation, the ecstasy in the human body: the climax; in symbolism, the flame.

## Previous Character of the Man—Intellectual, Moral and Physical: ...is an important element...

This mark of the cosmic sense is difficult to respond to with respect to oneself. Therefore, it must be addressed on behalf of my upbringing and family.

Since early childhood, without giving it much thought, I believe that I attempted to do what was right, which in the formative years probably means "what was expected of me." This early advantage was certain to have been derived from my parents' great care and example.

Dad and Mom never fought; never criticized. They possessed wonderful qualities, were responsible, honest, and forthright; they were exceedingly accepting, and provided a stable foundation in which to grow. Both were fair and even-tempered. During my adulthood, my father told me his philosophy was, "Always say 'yes' whenever possible."

Once at the county fair, when I was a child, a barker offered Dad a free comb. Dad did not take it, and when we left I asked him why. As near as I can recall, he said something like, "Because I did not earn it." To me at the time, that was no reason: I simply did not understand his perspective. After all, the comb was free. This incident made a permanent impression. I learned from it.

## A Tiny But Radiant Light

While teaching me to drive, he said, "Just remember, if you are on snow or ice, do not spin your wheels. If you are moving forward, even very slowly, you are making progress." Even at that age it impressed me, and I have applied it in an untold number of situations throughout life.

At a family reunion a few years after my father's death, his younger brother said of him, "He was the best engineer I ever knew." This nonchalant, unexpected comment swelled and enlightened my heart. Mother was warmhearted, thoughtful, attentive and loyal. I loved her laughter. She was always happy; her presence assured the cohesion and joy within our family.

Physically, we were all healthy, intellectually about average: with the exception that my father would occasionally comment that he believed my youngest brother was a genius.

Over a long adult lifetime, I did not always do the right thing. There were an untold number of mistakes and blunders; many were intentional, wherein I knew better.

**Age of Illumination: ...Should we hear of a case of cosmic consciousness occurring at twenty... we should at first doubt the truth... and if forced to believe it we should expect the man (if he lived) to prove himself...a veritable spiritual giant.**

Bucke proved that the majority of the forty persons whom he identified as possessing cosmic consciousness, or who showed obvious marks of the cosmic sense, were illumined in their thirties. Based upon the statistics, which he gathered and by comparing the illumination date when known with the length of the lifetime, he came to believe that they were illumined at their height of maturity.

Illumination or enlightenment may or may not have been attained to the level recognized by Bucke. However, the experience of the evening at a minimum granted the predawn to the twilight; notwithstanding, it was endowed to an essential degree. Here, it is called embrightenment, a silly term, but conceivably appropriate.

The oldest person entering into illumination was Emanuel Swedenborg at age 54. Second to Swedenborg was an unidentified woman who reached illumination at age 40. Embrightenment arrived at age 52. (Endnote 17).

Bucke also determined that most men and women reached illumination in the early spring, in May or June. Out of the twenty persons in whom Bucke was able to establish the time of year of their illumination, two persons were illumined in July; one person was illumined during the summer and three were between September and November. The embrightenment occurred in July.

**Added Charm to the Personality so that Men and Women are Always (?) Strongly Attracted to the Person: ...it is believed...**

Unfortunately, I am not able to speak to the extent of "charm" or lack thereof. About the only plus that can be added is, during my lifetime, there have been tremendous hurdles or mountains to traverse, similar to those of all other persons, and there have been strenuous flood and ebb tides. Despite that fact, I have been especially happy.

Even with respect to the detrimental decline, there was an inward joy which conflicted and battled its way to the forefront and succeeded. It seemed that the Detrimental Decline huddled groaning in the shadows and, in part, the Joy spurt forth-ward, a spotlight into the outward life. A monumental exception occurred after the horrendous death of my mother, when I was age 31; everything in me had to *fight back* after that blow.

There have been many unique statements, such as this one by a woman living in St. Clair Shores, Michigan, "Even the sky opens up to you." Other examples include a recent comment from a woman in Memphis, "God is looking out for *you*." and another from a wonderful and inspiring friend in Arkansas, who said, "You are one of the blessings of my life," and due to our numerous conversations and mutual respect, I understood that it was meant with respect to the spiritual realm.

(A word of warning: the personal ego immediately attempts to latch unto statements of this nature to magnify its perception of self. This elevation must be actively persistently tramped down. One must affirmatively keep in mind that any virtue one may receive, or of which is currently in at least temporary possession, belongs strictly to the divine within, and must not, shall not, be glorified to one's individual self.)

At some point in their life, all persons have traversed the hurdles, scaled the mountain tops, and strived with the flood and ebb tides. To this new prophetic sense, our striving is not in vain.

**Transformation…as Seen by Others…: There seems…to be sufficient evidence…with cosmic consciousness, while it is actually present… (gradually passing away) …a change takes place in the appearance…similar to that caused…by great joy…**

Once again, I am unable to speak directly to this mark of the cosmic sense. I did attempt to describe the transformation which occurred immediately at the moment of that evening, and which lasted one solid week, in the poem *In Simplicity and Stillness Sat* which is located in the section *New Life Living Within*.

This poem does not respond particularly well to the mark being addressed as the mark of the cosmic sense pertains to the exterior natural appearance. The poem is written from the perspective of the subsequent modification of the demeanor, and the notable alteration or transformation of the interior being. The poem primarily focuses on the indwelling pure placid calm.

There is one verified incident which does appear to meet Bucke's standard of "transformation of the subject of the change as seen by others when the cosmic sense is actually present." That event occurred many years later, with the receipt of the vision, the notification, of Ira's death, and lasted several days.

Specifically, two days after Ira's death and the informative vision, when looking in the mirror, I was astonished to see a familiar, but a younger version of myself. The few wrinkles appeared to be smoothed out. The face appeared reddish and extraordinarily healthy and vibrant. The mind was in awe of the image. It was apparent that the transformation was as a result of the ultra-brief encounter with, exposure to, or connection with, the source of the vision.

Moreover, upon entering the funeral home, an acquaintance greeted me with a surprising "Hello, good looking." The quizzical look and tone also told me that what was seen was also a surprise to him. Never had the person made a remark similar to that in the past. And, let's face it, no one says "good looking" to a person nearing age 70. Another said, "You look better than I have ever seen you look. Seriously, you do." Even I had been astonished by the difference in appearance, but here it was verified by two independent persons, one right after the other.
What happened? Why were those few days different?

(The vision of Ira's death was previously described in *To Breach the Gap—You are the Living Life within the Living Life*.)


**Added Consciousness: (Endnote 18) ...the new faculty instructs it without any new experience or process of learning. ...it acquires enormously increased powers of accumulating knowledge and of initiating action.**

Certain *things* were revealed by virtue of the mystical enlightenment or twilight and as a result are decidedly known; an insight was imbued which included an in-birthed knowledge or instruction. Of chief enormity in this instance is the keen sense of immortality as reconfirmed through the subsequent visions.

Wherever there is a vision, there is a source of the vision: and, this source is much higher and deeper, supernal, remarkably more majestic, than one can imagine or account for in one's own finite manner.

## A Tiny But Radiant Light

**Added Faculty: ...that the universe is not a dead machine but a living presence; ...in its essence and tendency it is infinitely good; ...individual existence is continuous beyond what is called death. He takes on enormously greater capacity both for learning and initiating.**

To my recollection, one precise explicit sense of the universe not being a dead machine but a living harmonious presence was instilled with the vision which is described in the poem titled the *Embodiment of Harmony*, in *Megan's Story*.

A second example is the phenomenal awareness of the Presence living co-jointly with the Calm and inhabiting the body in varying intensity for periods on end. The common distinction between these two examples is that they both speak to and exist within the Calm.

That the individual existence is continuous beyond death was revealed and observed clearly in the personal visions, and is stressed in the poems titled *Opened by An Unseen Hand* and *Never the Flame to Darken Out*.

After enlightenment, as previously asserted, there is an inborn knowledge of eternal life, which in turn is reflected in one's activities, and which enhances the basic understanding of the outer world. The inward knowledge is brought outward and the two are conjoined.

For my part, I am unable to determine whether there is an increased capacity for learning, as Bucke indicated in reference to the historical change, the significant change, from single to self-consciousness and also from self-consciousness to cosmic consciousness. Definitely, there is an unshakable capacity for initiating action. There is an overwhelming desire even now, seventeen years later, to speak forth that which was made known.

The knowledge gained surrounding and succeeding the mystical experience, simply cannot "die" with man. It knows, *itself,* that it must be sustained. It knows itself to be relevant. Beyond this, there is no further way to effectively elaborate. Perhaps the poetry speaks far more than for its selfsame purpose.

# CHAPTER X
# Endnotes

Endnote 1
Bucke, Richard Maurice, M.D. *Cosmic Consciousness, A Study in the Evolution of the Human Mind*, with an Introduction by George Moreby Acklom, New York, E. P. DUTTON AND COMPANY, INC., Publishers: Introduction is dated New York City, February 25, 1946. 14th Edition, 1948.
Note: Cosmic Consciousness may be found in the public domain on the Internet.

Endnote 2
Bucke, Richard Maurice, M.D., *Cosmic Consciousness. A Study in the Evolution of the Human Mind*, E.P. Dutton and Company, Inc.: a paperback edition, first published 1969 by E.P. Dutton and Co., Inc., Copyright 1901 by Innes & Sons, Copyright 1922 by Edward P.A. Connaughton, Copyright 1923 by E. P. Dutton and Company.

Endnote 3
Bucke, Richard Maurice, M.D. *Cosmic Consciousness, A Study in the Evolution of the Human Mind*, with an Introduction by George Moreby Acklom, New York, E. P. DUTTON AND COMPANY, INC., Publishers: Introduction is dated New York City, February 25, 1946. 14th Edition, 1948, p 3-4.

Endnote 4
Series II, Vol. 12, pp 159-196.

Endnote 5
Bucke, Richard Maurice, M.D. *Cosmic Consciousness, A Study in the Evolution of the Human Mind*, with an Introduction by George Moreby Acklom, New York, E. P. DUTTON AND COMPANY, INC., Publishers: Introduction is dated New York City, February 25, 1946. 14th Edition, 1948, Part I, *First Words*, pp 9-10.

## A Tiny But Radiant Light

Endnote 6
Bucke, Richard Maurice, M.D. *Cosmic Consciousness, A Study in the Evolution of the Human Mind*, with an Introduction by George Moreby Acklom, New York, E. P. DUTTON AND COMPANY, INC., Publishers: Introduction is dated New York City, February 25, 1946. 14$^{th}$ Edition, 1948. *John Yepes*, p 147.

Endnote 7
Ibid. ,IX, *From Self to Cosmic Consciousness*, pp 72-79.

Endnote 8
Ibid., IX, p 76.

Endnote 9
*Walt Whitman a Life* by Justin Kaplan, SIMON AND SCHUSTER – NEW YORK, Chapter 2, p 37.

Endnote 10
Only the barest of Bucke's sense is touched upon in this endeavor. It is essential to read Cosmic Consciousness to gain the vast insight in its entirety.

Endnote 11
Bucke, Richard Maurice, M.D. *Cosmic Consciousness, A Study in the Evolution of the Human Mind*, with an Introduction by George Moreby Acklom, New York, E. P. DUTTON AND COMPANY, INC., Publishers: Introduction is dated New York City, February 25, 1946. 14$^{th}$ Edition, 1948, *Marks of Cosmic Sense* delineated pp 72-75.

Endnote 12
I call this physical location the Second Center, or the Central Core, i.e. the second brought to light, meaning brought to *discovery* to the natural mind and to the physical body, but it is analogous to the first in nature: this generation is positively known.

The second center (which is actually the first, or primary center) is solely for the commission of the spiritual, the divine, the infinite to unite in spontaneity in an instant with the finite, the physical, to merge the qualities. The first center to be discovered, generally in young adulthood, is strictly a result of the conjugation of the finite to the finite.

Endnote 13

The energy transference could best be described by considering the child's toy wherein several spheres are suspended side-by-side each by their own string. When one lifts and drops one sphere it falls and transfers its momentum to the next one or more stationary spheres. Then the momentum derived from the first sphere bounces the final sphere outward with the original thrust of energy and the initial sphere stops immediately. (There was the conferment of the thrumming, then, concurrently the winds were no more.)

Endnote 14

Murry, J. Middleton, *God*, New York and London, Harper & Brothers Publishers, 1929, *Mysticism and After*, § 12, p 66, spoke of the Soul "being aware of the universe as a harmony and of itself as a part of that harmony; and this awareness was a joyful awareness."

In his lengthy technical analysis of the mystical experience, located in the second half of his book, the question is to discover "whether the mystical experience is illusion or truth" [p 122], Murry concludes of the harmony, "There is an attainable harmony in Man, and there is a harmony in the Universe, and there is a harmony between these two harmonies: one is dependent upon the other." Ibid, § 12, p 173.

Endnote 15

An appreciative account by Yogi Raushan Nath, THE UNSEEN HAND, A handbook of yoga way of life for self-realization, YOGI RAUSHAN NATH, Forward by DR. KARAN SINGH, RAJIV PUBLICATIONS, NEW DELHI, June 1971. Distributors: Trimuri Publications, W-152, Greater Kailash-I, New Delhi-48. PRINTED IN INDIA BY: NEW INDIA PRESS, K-BLOCK, CONNAUGHT CIRCUS, NEW DELHI-1. THE EIGHTFOLD PATH OF YOGA, CONSCIENCE: YOGA REVIEWS IT, p 129.

Man is yet in the making. He may beget himself another sense-organ for the conscience as well. For all we know, it may already be in the making.

Human consciousness does not talk as talking goes. But the conscience does speak out. You can hear its voice—not in a dream but while awake.

The voice of the conscience is a unique experience. It has no physical cause—it is Anahata. Unlike our speech, no part of the body is involved in voicing it.

## A Tiny But Radiant Light

Sometimes, I feel that it's the collective urge, emanating from the great ones, that surges forward to put man on the right path. Their sense of responsibility towards him finds a voice! Once I saw it all in a vision sublime.

Endnote 16
*Goes Its Way A* Cautioning and *Macro Goal* appear in the Appendix.

Endnote 17
Bucke, Richard Maurice, M.D. *Cosmic Consciousness, A Study in the Evolution of the Human Mind*, with an Introduction by George Moreby Acklom, New York, E. P. DUTTON AND COMPANY, INC., Publishers: Introduction is dated New York City, February 25, 1946. 14th Edition, 1948, p 81.

Endnote 18
Ibid., IX, p 75-76

# CHAPTER XI

## JOHN MIDDLETON MURRY—"An Experience That Enabled Me to Understand"

In the Preface of *God*, (Endnote 1) the author, John Middleton Murry, explains that this is a queer yet simple book and determines that the title should be simple, *God*, rather than a more elaborate and forbidding one such as *An Introduction to the Science of Metabiology*. An unidentified partial newspaper clipping, which was pasted to the inside front cover of my copy of *God*, reads, "His (Murry's) volume constitutes an intimate spiritual autobiography as well as a stimulating guide to the searching mind of contemporary man." (Endnote 2)

\*\*\*

John Middleton Murry, a celebrated intellectual, well-known literary critic and prolific writer of the early twentieth century, suffered a severe loss in the early years of his young marriage as a result of the short illness and sudden death of his wife, Katherine Mansfield Murry. This devastating event imposed an agonizing struggle which he was neither able to comprehend nor to contend. Murry could barely endure the conflict between his benumbed mind and his non-accepting non-understanding heart.

He described his personal circumstance, his frame of mind after her death, as "I had come to the end of my tether. I had reached a point of total dereliction and despair. I call it total; it was not quite total, as will appear, but relatively to any condition of mind that I had experienced before, it was an 'irrecoverably dark, total eclipse.'" (Endnote 3)

## A Tiny But Radiant Light

At that dreary point in his life Murry realized that he was not clear on "what he intended to do" to permit himself to wholly grasp reality; to culminate in the continuance of a bearable life. Yet instinctively he knew enough to search for the quietude and solitude with which to grapple with the intolerable situation.

As a result, he set the scene which would best allow him to convince his self-conscious mind that he was alone; to accept the death of his beloved wife, Katherine. In his naivete, in his desperation, he was led to establish the conditions which, unbeknown to him at the time, could conceivably engender a birthing of at least partial illumination.

\*\*\*

Let us begin to peer over Murry's shoulder to perceive a second-hand view of the landscape from his poignant perspective beginning shortly after the death of Katherine Mansfield.

Perceptively, fortunately, Murry, in a memorandum to himself, memorialized the astounding moments of the mysterious spiritual experience; this detail was written within three to four months of the experience while the emotion and feeling were still fresh in his mind. This enlightened man could not have presented his case more succinctly or more thoughtfully than in those few descriptive paragraphs, located in Section Seven of *God*. (Endnote 4)

"'Really alone.' I meant something by it, something more than could be achieved by the mere act of going off to a remote cottage in a Sussex forest and living by myself...I had not even the faintest notion of what I should, or could do..."

Then "in the dark, in the dead, still house" Murry sat motionless facing the fire. He focused his attention and tried for what seemed to be hours to convince himself that he was alone. "Prompted by some instinct," he "tried to force his consciousness into every part of" his "body." Slowly, he succeeded. At last, he "had the sensation that" he '*was* in' his "hands and feet" and "there at a frontier" of his "being," he ended. Then "stretched out vast immensities, of space, the universe...something that was other" than himself. It was utterly unknown to him. At last he could "gaze steadily." He "became aware of himself as a little island against whose slender shores a cold, dark, boundless ocean lapped devouring. Somehow in that moment" he "knew that" he "had reached a pinnacle of personal being."

Near that point in his narrative, John Middleton Murry made the most mysterious, and what would on-the-surface seem to be a low-key benign statement, a statement which one would normally pass over without the blink of an eye or a hesitation in thought, "What happened then? If I could tell that, I should tell a secret indeed."

Murry explained in breathtaking detail that "a moment came when the darkness of that ocean…changed to light…it swept in one great wave over the shores and frontiers of" himself "it bathed" and he "was renewed…when the room was filled with a presence…" and he knew he was "not alone…" He knew he never could be alone any more…" He "was part of it" He "*belonged.*" (Endnote 5)

In the remote cottage in Sussex forest, an unexpected powerful spiritual experience took place which brought about "a feeling of 'serene illumination.'"

\*\*\*

All facets of Murry's mystical experience, together with its aftereffects, including the consequential influence into the activities of his physical, mental, emotional and spiritual life, surprised and astonished him. The subsequent interaction of the manifestation swayed his natural thought process and challenged his lifelong beliefs. His relationship with his friends and business partner were severely altered; he reoriented his life. He was "a new man."

His belief that the effects were both beneficial and non-beneficial, and his need to thoroughly understand, led Murry to the very "thing" that he does best. It led him to undertake a complex critical analysis of the nature of the entire event and process and of the life-long implications.

# A Tiny But Radiant Light

As a result, in 1929, six years after Mansfield's death in 1923, Murry published his very intriguing informative book, *God*: Part I is autobiographical; Part II includes, *The New Man, Mysticism and After,* and other pertinent titles. In his autobiography, he candidly delineated the major aspects of their troubled married life from several months prior to the onset of Mansfield's illness.

He elaborated on the events, circumstances, and heightened emotions surrounding her death, and dwelled on the heart-wrenching aftermath. Further, he effectively elucidated pertinent events of his childhood.

Perceptively, I believe, for future generations, he thoroughly documented his thought process. Murry especially honed in on that which had been dramatically and spontaneously altered. He was now in a vastly greater possession of spiritual knowledge than before.

The autobiographical Part I of his impressive book is human and warm, leisurely reading. It seems to be written essentially from a gentle-loving heart.

Part II seems to be written by a cool analytical professional standing at arm's-length, and stoically removed emotionally. He evaluated each facet of the spiritual experience and its ramifications as if he were a critical outsider looking in.

## Equivalent Elements of the Illumination and Embrightenment Experience
(Endnote 6)

The "natural and inevitable" procedure, followed by Murry in his self-defined irrecoverably dark period with its unendurable desolation, springs to mind the near identical circumstance of the comparable dank period of the *Deepest, Darkest Shadow and Despair* suffered after the death of my mother. The colossal distinction between the immediate consequences of the two experiences is that Murry's attempt "to force the consciousness into..." immediately culminated in illumination, in a rendering of the cosmic sense.

Contrarily, the period of deepest, darkest shadow and despair, the solitude and concentration while sitting on the end of the bed in the attempt to "locate" my mother (the intentional concentration, of reaching *out* to a *lost* loved one), secured access to a momentary, foreshadowing, mental region. It did not constitute the immediate embrightenment experience, yet it foreshadowed and propelled a destined spiritual pathway (Endnote 7). Now, let us permanently set aside, the "concentration while sitting at the end of the bed." Yet, let us note that both experiences were preceded by a devastating event; the death of a loved one.

Notwithstanding, and here is the crux: of eminent significance are the greater commonalities between Murry's natural and inevitable procedure in the cottage in Sussex shortly following the death of Mansfield and my determination in search of a potential foreseeable inspirational or spiritual awakening a distant 22 years after the death of my mother.

That evening, I was instinctively led to stay awake all night, to read the works of Walt Whitman, until "something," something spiritual, happened. Past experience had shown that prolonged reading of Whitman's *Leaves of Grass* would induce an alluring sympathetic rhythm which would affect the body and mind in a comforting soothing manner. This second attempt to reach into the unknown startlingly climaxed in embrightenment, as Murry's first attempt immediately culminated in illumination. These two experiences are generally equivalent in nature.

Unlike Murry, whose mystical illumination was apparently ignited unexpectedly and spontaneously and with little to no knowledge of the likelihood of illumination afore hand. At that same juncture I understood clearly that there was the potential for an inspirational experience or a spiritual awakening of an extraordinary nature, or at least for "something," as set forth previously in *Recognition of Something Soon to Occur*.

These are the experiences of two everyday people; though, indeed, Murry was a well-known intellectual who possessed the capability and the natural inclination to definitively analyze the experience and to set forth his conclusions in a coherent manner.

## A Tiny But Radiant Light

Murry's book, *God*, as-well-as the heartfelt affirmations contained in the inspired poetry, presented in this factual narrative, describe direct true-life mystical experiences.

The outpourings stand forthright in their own upright position; they bear credence that the genuine illumination experience, secured or endowed is advantageous and forever affects and influences the being, his/her life, thought, demeanor and action. And, based solely on personal experience, I believe that I am safely able to affirm that it enhances one's health. It also affects a gratifying lightheartedness and levity.

\*\*\*

The following constitutes a comparison of equivalent elements of the illumination experience with those of the embrightenment experience, together with a few of the lingering gifts.

With respect to Murry, the comparison will primarily focus on the information contained in the autobiographical section of *God*, which contains a comprehensive description of Murry's mood and state of mind surrounding the circumstances leading up to and including the phenomenal illumination experience, rather than on the succeeding analysis delineated in Part II.

With respect to the evening of the embrightenment, the comparison will both repeat and augment former information.

The five categories that follow are either perhaps newly identified as an unendurable sorrow, or are generally broadened from the thirteen marks of cosmic sense as defined by Bucke: The purpose of this "unbearable sorrow" is to bring to light the potential effect a drastic shock or devastating event may have on the potential for a mystical experience.

**Unbearable Sorrow**
    **—Circumstances, or Motivating Factors,**
**Preceding the Mystical Experience**
      **—A Shock;**
      **—Natural and Inevitable Procedure,**
**Subsequent to the Death of a Loved One;**

**Marks of the Cosmic Sense**
    **—Elements of the Actual Mystical,**
**Illumination, Embrightenment, Experience**
      **—An Adjoining;**
      **—A New Man;**
      **—Alteration of Life;**

In the delineation below, the individual category, or circumstance, is listed first; thereafter, presented is a partial extract of one or more of the related elements of Murry's illumination experience followed by the precise statement, the gilded thread, contained in Murry's *Autobiography* regarding the "pinnacle experience" (Endnote 8).

Finally listed is at least one kindred statement or related equivalent element, pertaining directly to the evening's embrightenment experience; comments may follow.

        **Unbearable Sorrow:**
          **—A Shock**

**Murry—Katherine Mansfield's Death—a Shock to the Spiritual…I was Numbed**
    **Background**
        When Murry was a young boy playing cricket with another youngster, he recalls, "the sky seemed to fall on top of my head, and I was felled to the ground." The other young person "had been struck by lightning, and was dead." Murry states, "As was the shock of that lightning

flash to the physical part of me, so was the shock to Katherine Mansfield's death to the spiritual."

**Equivalent Element**

In December of 1969, Mom died suddenly with nearly no forewarning. The surgeon's knife accidentally slipped and cut the main artery down her back. She immediately went into shock from the loss of blood. In the attempt to bring her out of shock she aspirated, burning out her lungs within weeks.

I believed that I could not go on without her, at least without reaching her; her loss was so acute, so staunch, so severe.

**Comment**

Years prior to Katherine Mansfield's death, Murry was exposed to a severe shock caused by witnessing the sudden death of his young boyhood friend; he does not describe the nature of the shock or the probable emotional effect, however he reports on the happening. Many years prior to the evening of the embrightenment, I was to receive a severe shock by the sudden death of my mother.

Each set of circumstances projected long forecasted shadows into the being of these two individuals and into the future. The long forecasted shadows are confirmed in Murry's case as the sudden and tragic death of his young friend was still prevalent in his mind at the time of his writing the book, *God*; he intentionally set-forth the details in his autobiography.

Obviously, a dramatic cause, and the imposed endurance of a drastic effect of this nature, is not requisite to a mystical experience. However, these two instances, plus the discovery, according to Murry, that the poet John Keats "had undergone a kindred desolation" caused by the illness and death of Keats "dearly loved" brother, George, and Murry's realization that he, Murry, had received a kindred illumination, is cause for further consideration.

Murry quotes Keats, "Oh, Brown, I have coals of fire in my heart. It surprises me that the human heart is capable of containing and bearing so much misery." (Endnote 9) All three persons were constrained to endure the heart-wrenching effect of the death of their loved one.

## Unbearable Sorrow:
## Natural and Inevitable Procedure, Subsequent to the Death of a Loved One

### Murry—Compelled to Search for Solitude

Subsequent to the death of Mansfield, Murry felt that "the condition" he "was in was degrading for a human being…" He "must go away…and be really alone—really alone."

### Equivalent Element

Perhaps an *undeveloped* intuition also drew me to solemnity, to the quietude of this moment, of this evening. I had previously read or heard of situations regarding other persons, themselves embroiled in gloomy desperation, reaching out to loved ones on the *uttermost* side.

### Comment

Murry felt the necessity to go to a remote cottage to seek the solitude which he deemed necessary, while I merely sought solitude within my own home.

### Murry—Compelled to Explore

He knew he was required to do something…such as "take a plunge into the unknown." It was as if he "were being compelled to explore a dark cave alone." He had

not the faintest notion of what he should, or could, do."
He "had no hesitations."

**Equivalent Element**
A pivotal night a few weeks or months after my mother's death, a pure unbearable accumulative sorrow and dreadful despair plagued and permeated my being. Fervent intention compelled me to try, in my non-knowing how, now, to reach her, to grasp into the beyond.


**Murry—Forced the Consciousness**
"At that moment it was natural and inevitable that I should have tried to force the consciousness that I was physically alone into every part of my body…It came natural to me in my extremity."

**Equivalent Element**
I could feel there was the potential for an inspirational experience or a spiritual awakening, albeit, nothing as grand as pure enlightenment, just *something*, merely something! The intuitive knowledge was alert and valid. I was inwardly driven by measures considerably beyond my active earthly comprehension.


## Marks of the Cosmic Sense:
## —An Adjoining

**Murry—Dark/Darkness; Boundless Ocean Lapped; Pinnacle of Personal Being; What Happened Then? If I could tell that, I should tell a secret indeed…**
"Yet out upon this from the fragile rampart of my own body, I found the courage to peer, to glance, at last to gaze steadily. And I became aware of myself as a little island against whose slender shores a cold, dark, boundless ocean lapped devouring. Somehow

in that moment I knew that I had reached a pinnacle of person being."

### Equivalent Element—of the Evening and Moment: Dark/Darkness; Boundless Ocean Lapped

I had been abruptly awakened to an intensity of sound, the loud thunderous raging of swiftly rushing winds, breaking through the darkness, surging toward me, striking and spontaneously infusing me with its unique sympathetic rhythm: a surcharge—a sudden enkindling, a burst with its immense crowning intimate-pulsation in the middle of the head toward the top, thence flaring or flashing upward slightly over the head, then downward toward the shoulders. Then, slowly, perceptively, the pronounced pulsing sensation spread out through the arms, into the hands and fingers and began to edge down the chest...The movement, the traveling of the striking physical manifestation...all striking pulsation... (The enkindling with its traveling ecstasy... Endnote 10)

### Comment: Dark/Darkness

Murry chose the identical word "dark" in conjunction with the prelude to the "boundless ocean lapped devouring," which overcame him—devouring, which "took-him-in,"—just prior to reaching the "pinnacle of personal being."

It appears that the word dark was used intentionally in an unequivocal visual/physical sense and that it was not meant in a brooding mental or emotional sense. It is extremely curious, and unquestionably no coincidence, that the breaking through the darkness played such a staunch role in the accelerated delivery of both the pinnacle experience and of the mystical embrightement experience.

Three to four months after the actual spiritual experience when Murry wrote of his account in the memorandum to himself, the "dark" was relegated insignificantly into the background. I, too, held little recognition of the darkness until it smacked me in the face when addressing the issue of the Subjective Light noted above in the section on Bucke, but, lo-and-behold, it was only recognized for its infinite worth when elaborated upon below in this section of Murry when addressing the Subjective Light.

The winds and the physical sensation, in conjunction with the alertness of mind of the embrightenment experience, had so overshadowed the darkness, that although the darkness remained prominent in the sight of the memory (the picture etched within the mind), for years its actual crucial relevance received no overt recognition or attention, whatsoever. This seems unbelievable that the significance of the dark/darkness was not consciously recognized sooner.

**Comment: Boundless Ocean Lapped**

Murry's "boundless ocean lapped devouring..." corresponds precisely to the "swiftly rushing winds," spontaneously infusing their unique sympathetic rhythm.

The "winds" convey/instill the selfsame message/affect, as Murry's "boundless ocean."All rhythmic and pulsating physical sensations of the embrightenment relate directly to "lapped," waves overlapping. *Lapped* repeats. It is a repetition; a rhythm, a cadence, a pulsing.

The "devouring" Murry mentions incorporates the entire engulfing of the enbrightenment from the point of impact, the burst within the head, to the annihilating thought.

**Murry—Pinnacle of Personal Being;**
**—What Happened Then?**
**—If I could tell that, I should tell a secret indeed...**

"Somehow in that moment I knew that I had reached a pinnacle of person being. I was I, as I had never been before—and never should be again. It was strange that I should have known that; but then I did know it, and it was not strange. What happened then? If I could tell that, I should tell a secret indeed."

**Comment**

Murry reached a pinnacle of person being; he is as he has never been before. He does not indicate what happens then. However, he states "If I could tell that, I should tell a secret indeed." This is the most subtle, the most essential and illuminating, statement that he could have made. Vague and elusive as it is, this sentence alerts one to a further deeper secret; a grand knowledge of a moment of the event, of which he did not elaborate

Think of it! Out of 344 pages in *God*, this instance, this precise moment, is merely mentioned in passing. Every other item/issue, process or sequence, in relation to this mystical experience was thoroughly assessed and addressed between the covers of his book.

*Something* happened—Murry pointed to a secret, a mystery, so vast and so unbelievable—something of which, he undoubtedly would not or could not overtly reveal, perhaps, in minor part, due to the incompatibility with the inhibition of his generation.

Secondarily and most importantly, to the best of my expectation based upon my knowledge, Murry's experience was so personal as it approached and pervaded his physical body that one heartily wonders at the incredulity of the physical feeling.

This, I clearly understand. The ancient mystics speak of an "ecstasy": The mystics are precise. The experience, itself, breeds a strenuous caution not to be indiscriminately divulged; It recognizes Itself to be sacred. The recipient may never openly express its exact nature.

There is one succinct statement in the analytical second part of *God* where once again Murry addresses this hallowed moment of enlightenment. He says, "He (Jesus) taught men how to prepare for the joyful consummation of the Reign of God, by achieving within themselves the same intimate experience of God which had come to him." (Endnotes 11, 12) It is evident that the word "themselves" in Murry's statement also applies to Murry's personal mystical experience.

The last sentence in the above paragraph is fortified by the assertion that there was an actual "pinnacle" of the mystical experience, "If I could tell that, I should tell a secret indeed." It further explains why Murry realized that he had "...an experience that enabled me to understand..." (Endnotes 13, 14) In another location he states "...and I also believe that we have the faculty of recognizing instantly when another has achieved this consummation." (Endnote 15)

His use of the terms "joyful consummation, intimate experience," and "achieved this consummation," provide an open, yet hidden, clue to the exact nature of the manifestation of the enlightenment experience. (Yet, continue to remember, there may be significant variation in degree.)

Embrightenment (the enkindling), too, does not precisely address the "What happened then." It provides a grand description of the process, the nature of the traveling of the feeling, the accompanying thought, but of the precise moment it states: The only current, yet unequivocal, imposing or compelling-prompting is to set forth the mystical experience in its undivided merit; in clarity; in its entirety in one cohesive whole. Still, the precise mode of ignition—the enkindling—hinted at, is left to the reader to discover for himself or herself. The enkindling is beyond laudable and is worth the lifetime to secure.

**Murry—Swept in one great wave over the shores and frontiers of myself, when it bathed me and I was renewed**

"But a moment came when the darkness of that ocean changed to light, the cold to warmth, when it swept in one great wave over the shores and frontiers of myself, when it bathed me and I was renewed."

**Equivalent Element**

...the loud thunderous raging of swiftly rushing winds... surging... striking and spontaneously infusing... with their unique sympathetic rhythm: a surcharge—a sudden enkindling of the physical—the uniting—in stunned awe.

**Comment**

It appears that Murry's "boundless ocean," in one great singular wave (of many [lapped], if there was an accompanying rhythm [Which to my knowledge and experience, there must be a rhythm if he achieved illumination]), represents the same undulating rhythm as the embrightenment's thunderous raging of "swiftly rushing winds," (Represented in this instance, only, as plural [winds], which plurality would produce the vibratory component of sound. [But *Winds* is definitely single in *its* being. It, the "winds," is one.]) with winds' intensity, striking and spontaneously infusing the winds' sympathetic rhythm: a surcharge—a sudden enkindling, a burst, (Murry says, *Explosion*. Endnote 16) with its immense intimate-pulsation.

To repeat the paragraph above without the interruptions: It appears that Murry's "boundless ocean," in one great singular wave represents the same undulating rhythm as the embrightenment's thunderous raging of "swiftly rushing winds," with winds' intensity, striking and spontaneously infusing the winds' sympathetic rhythm: a surcharge—a sudden enkindling, a burst, with its immense intimate-pulsation.

In an instant, the thunderous winds' *pulsation* was conveyed to the physical, the enkindling of the physical—the uniting. The pulsation swept, traveled, engulfed. The Mind "watched" in stunned awe.

(On a major, yet divergent note, Murry makes no mention of what was so overpowering and prominent in the embrightenment, sound. He makes no mention of sound!)

Murry's "When it bathed me and I was renewed..." also corresponds to the effect of the embrightenment; "To the common consciousness it loves, it glows, without apparent reason, for its own inevitable purpose. It unites with the *individual*; ameliorates the individual. It appears to shine forth from within and propels the *two*, now one, forth-ward in continuity, in generosity."


**Murry—Room was filled with a Presence; Universe beyond held no menace for I was part of it...I belonged...**

"...when the room was filled with a presence, and I knew I was not alone—that I never could be alone any more, that the universe beyond held no menace, for I was part of it, that in some way for which I had sought in vain so many years, I *belonged*...

Where I say that "the room was filled with a presence," the "presence" was definitely connected with the person of Katherine Mansfield. I do not mean that the room was filled with her "presence"; but that her "presence" was given to my consciousness simultaneously with the "presence" that filled the room."

**Equivalent Element: Room was Filled with a Presence**
The initial reference in this current work cites the Presence as contemporaneous with four other gifts: a suffused sacred Calm, a laudable Presence; a riotous bounteous Joy, a Youth within; and an abounding prolific Eternal Love, a love beyond earthly comprehension and description.

**Comment**
However, Murry's reference is clear. He describes and explains the presence in a differing manner, namely, as it relates to the *universal*—"the universe beyond...*I belonged*...for I was part of it."—and he speaks of the individual whom he loved—"the prese*n*ce was definitely connected with the person of Katherine Mansfield," whose presence, simultaneously given to his consciousness, "was of the same order as the 'presence' which filled the room..." and which filled him.

In Murry's description, the "presence" does not appear to extend over a period of many years. Yet it does. He was "convinced that all was well with her." And his mind is relieved: morally, he is relieved. The moral influence of this presence definitely did extend over time as it afforded him a *new* life; restored him, "to a life of the kind" he values.

The Presence of the embrightenment made itself prominent over a period, which extended into many years; there was never an identification with any individual. It associated itself with the Calm. Perhaps, the "Universal" in Murry's description is analogous to the "Calm."

**Equivalent Element: Universe Beyond Held No Menace, for I was Part of It...I belonged:**
Immediately, I wept silent, light tears, recognizing—a comprehension more grand than mere knowledge, a *Knowing,* a consciousness that this gift was, is, of divine origin. I rested blessed, rapt in the profound lingering

effects of the rhythm; of the newly formally instilled mild pulsation of a blessed calm; of an overflowing love; of an inborn sacred knowledge; of this majesty in ecstasy. The *Moment* of revelation dawned an unexpressible boundless Love, a love burgeoning outward.

Knowledge Known and Thunderous Sound are greater than twins. They are conjoined mates. The two cannot be subdivided. They are birthed together, just prior to (but, with no perceptible lapse in "time") the delivery—the strike—of the Enkindling; which enkindling implants that faculty which reigns supreme and which also awakens the individual to the knowledge of an everlasting life.

**Comment**
Thunderous Sound, the winds delivered the enkindling, which Enkindling, Itself, ignited, was the ignition, (the espousal of above and below—a conjunction of the infinite and the finite.) This conjunction of the infinite and the finite equates to Murry's "...the universe beyond held no menace, for I was part of it, that in some way for which I had sought in vain so many years, I belonged, and because I belonged I was no longer I, but something different, which could never be afraid in the old ways or cowardly with the old cowardice."

"I belonged..." Murry so simplified the immediate unifying effect of the illumination experience that even today it astounds me. This "belonged" is the adjoining, the espousal of the above, the infinite, and the below, the finite; the undivided marriage—the endowed and the gratefully received—an event so mysterious in its delivery, in the interaction, in the mind and body's immediate response, that no words will bear the load of conveyance to another. Murry says it best, "I belonged."

Margaret Mary Stender

## Marks of the Cosmic Sense
## A New Man

**Murry—I was no longer I, but something different**
Again: "a moment came when the darkness of that ocean changed to light, the cold to warmth; when it swept in one great wave over the shores and frontiers of myself, when it bathed me and I was renewed; when the room was filled with a presence, and I knew that I was not alone—that I could never be alone any more,...and because I belonged I was no longer I, but something different..."

Men who learned and obeyed it, became different. "They were a new kind of men." (Endnote 17)

...but I am constrained to recognize that the influence of the mystical experience is deep and in a sense ineradicable. It causes a deep and permanent change in one's mental dispositions. One becomes *convinced* of something, in a way in which one has never been *convinced* of anything, in heaven or earth, before, unless perhaps it be of the mere fact of one's own existence. (Endnote 18)

**Equivalent Element**
   Megan knew that there was, "No question that she was different
   From that point on. Not better, holier, or more sacred
     Just different..."

One simply is "the change," has already perceptually changed with the enkindling. One is a new creation; virtually a new man; one with the unity, the harmony, of the universe. He or she intuitively knows it!

## Comment

From the moment of the powerful spiritual experience forward, the individual is newborn never to revert completely to the old barbarian, and instantly abandoned, ways and theories: all prior perspective dramatically changes. Never again, would one be merely human: Bucke may have said the person is a case of cosmic consciousness; Murry may have said the person is a significant variation. Murry did inquire whether in that one "moment the veil of the hidden God was drawn." (Endnote 19)


## Marks of the Cosmic Sense
## Alteration of Life

**Murry—Impelled me into a course of action**
"It impelled me into a course of action which in a sense I still follow.

...it set my mind upon a chain of thinking which I have never relinquished; it restored me to life of the kind I value; and, indeed, it has occupied me ever since. ...Most of what I have thought or written since that night, and actually this book, have had its origin in the attempt to separate the truth and value of that experience from whatever elements of illusion, or potential illusion, it might contain." (Endnote 20)

**Equivalent Element**
This is the true story of one woman's mystical experience, perhaps ineptly told. She was blessed with the greatest of gifts: a blithe-full calm; a buoyant eternal love—Love Eternal—; a knowledge etched and impregnated withon her soul; a riotous bounteous joy; the Youth within; the Golden Glow; the prophetic visions; *the 180-degree radical transition of life*, and the necessity to

write in a poetical vein—to expound upon, applaud, and announce of the Gift inborn, instilled within;

...with the continual inner prompting, there re-arose the compelling desire to speak "aloud" once again. The writing resumed. Shortly, therein, I quit again for a period of several months. I quit several times and there were prolonged periods in between. Since the book remained active in my mind and by then heavily on my conscience, I eventually reduced the initial scope to what I considered possibly to be manageable and began once again.

One could conceptually be aware in advance, of the sudden 180-degree transformation in one's life, as a result of an experience of this nature. However, it is doubtful that one can conceive of the actual ennobling heftiness that the radical transformation *imposes*. In reality, the change constitutes an immediate substantive, conjoining, affirmative-shift.

**Comment**
With respect to the mystical experience itself, there was no illusion: truth was truth: the experience was exalted, and the reality was etched thoroughly within the mind, and, to my belief, withon or within the soul—etched, forever; amalgamated; one!

However, it is imperative to respond to Murry's statement concerning his perception of the separation of "the truth and value of that experience from whatever elements of illusion, or potential illusion, it might contain."

Considerably after the onset of the poetry, there was a certain amount of personal illusion. I believed that the engifted poetry or prose might be exploited in an undue non-productive manner. Even then, I was aware of the exaggerated eccentricity; yet the poetry was unduly protected.

Another area of potential illusion consists in the subject of "is there no conscience or is there no sin" wherein one believes to an extreme, or as propounded in Murry, that presumes a "fundamental rightness."

Having now brought this embarrassing confession forward, it is fitting to reiterate that the message propounded in this book is no illusion, but is pure in itself, is unyielding in its spirit to bring-to-light.

Sufficient time has elapsed, 17 years, in having lived with the infused knowledge; with the heightened, then mellowed emotions; with the persistent introspection; with the subdued temperament and demeanor; with transformed desires; with the distancing to the material world; with the instilled requisite to write; with the many years to rely on the gifts and on the knowledge endowed, to proclaim the surety of the message.

"*It* speaks of itself." As Yogi Raushan Nath, an acquaintance Indian Yogi, would say, "Sit down by my side in peace and with reverence for the Lord Who has chosen to give words to my lifelong sadhana. I was reluctant to let them face the callous indifference of the times. But the words? They did not heed my warning and called out to me over their shoulders: 'We will weather it all and shall triumph in the questing hearts that seek self-realization.'" (Endnote 21)

\*\*\*

Perhaps the following paragraphs concerning Murry and the alteration of life are unnecessary, yet because he changed so dramatically after illumination, the information may be pertinent. The comments begin in a negative, a near desperate manner (as one can well understand), but after illumination, they proceed in a positive tone with a new outlook on life.

Prior to Murry's marriage to Mansfield, Murry's tutor called him "inhuman." After marriage, with the horrendous ongoing events and effects of the war and the loss of friends of his own age, he felt there had been "a chasm created to yawn" in his universe.

He felt the "sick and grinding obsession" of the war; he was an "unbearable companion" with his "unshifting depression"; his "instinctive fear of life became a hatred and a terror." He felt "the world was mad"; he became depressed over Mansfield's illness and linked her illness with the feeling that it "...was as much a circumstance of the war as any death at the front." He was devoid of religion. These and numerous other circumstances augmented his unamenable condition, and propelled Murry into an emotional upheaval whereby he knew that he "had to find some fragment of a faith in life." (Endnote 22)

The above paragraph does not adequately convey that inordinate strain which Murry so emphatically stressed when speaking of his mental and emotional condition. Nor does it address any difficulties of his childhood. However, the point in laying out this dilemma is mainly to emphasize that, even before his marriage, Murry acknowledged that his tutor had called him inhuman, (Endnote 23) and that he had become "rankled," but more important, six plus years later, at the writing of the book, Murry believed that the tutor was right.

Thus, he acknowledged that his outlook may have needed significant improvement, not only before Mansfield's illness, complicated by the disastrous conditions of the war, but even prior to making her acquaintance. Yet, after illumination, after his new perspective, Murry proclaimed "a faith in life." He used the very words that he had previously used to describe his desperate condition before illumination, as having to find some fragment of a faith in life. This is important, in that, after the powerful spiritual experience, for months to years, he was virtually a new man.

***

A myriad of elements, thoughts and emotions, together with the experience preceding and subsequent to the death of Katherine Mansfield, is parallel to those described by Bucke; the similarities indicated below in Murry's work reflect the distinct marks of the cosmic sense.

As noted previously, Bucke identified and quoted the appropriate authority or quoted the original writings by each individual to arrive at his theories and conclusions. The authority for each case or instance of illumination is immortalized in Bucke's work in the idiom and metaphor of each individual's own period in history. However, the resemblance Murry presents is apparent in content and in context regardless of the slightly differing terminology and outlook on life.

Although Murry gave no indication that he had read or even heard of Bucke, he assuredly knew that he had undergone a form of the illumination experience. He spoke of mysticism throughout his work. He also referenced the illumination of at least three persons, for example "...the discovery that Keats had undergone a kindred desolation and received a kindred illumination was of great importance to me...I realized still more acutely, that 'illuminations' are troublesome experiences." And, in speaking of D. H. Lawrence, Murry said, "He was proclaiming the necessity of that absolute spiritual regeneration, that passing beyond the intellectual consciousness, which I in my fashion had experienced." (Endnotes 24, 25)

By virtue of his description, it is positively clear that he was a case of cosmic consciousness or at a bare minimum what Bucke would call a lesser or imperfect case, the twilight.

Many elements of Murry's experience relate to the marks of the cosmic sense, and should be outwardly acknowledged; these are delineated below, perhaps inclusive of an experience of the embrightenment, or of a comment.

**Subjective Light**

Murry paid especial heed to establish that "a moment came when the darkness changed to light, the cold to warmth...." He did not mention a color or the specific nature of the light, and one cannot state with absolute conclusion that Murry's light was identical, or even similar in nature, to Bucke's broad definition of the light. Murry does, however, recognize the presence of the light. This reference shows that he made a conscious effort to describe the contrast, the light and the "warmth;" a counterbalance to the darkness and cold, made a definite lasting impression.

What is equally crucial in this recognition is this light occurred just prior to his ultimate statement of "What happened then? If I could tell that, I should tell a secret indeed;" this "What happened then," as already mentioned, is the pinnacle of the manifestation of the powerful spiritual experience; his mystical revelation.

Murry also noted a second experience with the light. This *form of* light was present the morning following the spiritual experience. He stated, "I was not only convinced of the reality of my experience, but everything that I saw appeared to be radiant, not in the sense that it was suffused with an alien light, but as though every object that met my eyes were distinct with a rich and glorious distinctness which objects had never possessed for me before. This quality of vision remained with me for about a week, during which it gradually faded." (Endnote 26)

The recognition of the "second" light indicates there may be a type of an extension, or a related form of the initial subjective light—or enhanced faculty—which normally appears at the onset of the illumination experience, which extends into the period, according to Murry "about a week beyond" the spiritual experience. This may also indicate there is a temporary magnification of the physical sense to exterior light.

Previously, I stated that during the onset of the embrightenment experience "there was no true visual distinction, yet there was a clear perception. There was definitely a vertical obstructing aspect; still all was darkness; still with no light; visible yet non-visible in the ordinary sense. There was a distinguishing, but no light. No color." In this instance, the experience not only differs from that specified by Bucke in the marks of cosmic sense, but also differs from that of Murry.

However, I am definitely familiar with the secondary form of *light*, of vision—the form that Murry experienced the morning following the mystical experience. To the best of my recollection, it did not occur immediately following the embrightenment experience, but periodically caught me by surprise with its mien and astonishment in the days to years following. I could see to the treetops; every leaf was of vibrant color; I was astounded by being able to see the individual leaves clearly together with the whole scene; every detail stood out. I could see across the lake; every house was distinct and appeared much nearer than normal.

The clarity affected the mind in wondrous ways with a distinguished awe. While the sight was so unusually vibrant, the mind questioned its reality, particularity its cause (What is this wonderment?), yet recognized concurrently that it was not imagination. These rare periods of enhanced normal sight always occurred while out in the natural environment and lasted only for several enthralling minutes.

Another curious point is the coincidence of Murry's "This quality of vision remained with me for about a week" is precisely the identical time frame of my "...a full complete-absorbing calm rested within her being for one full week..." The question here is, "Was it truly a coincidence, or is this roughly seven days pertinent?"

**Intellectual Illumination**

Murry was an intellectual prior to the powerful spiritual experience, nevertheless, an intellectual illumination did take place. This is clearly evidenced by the content of the book *God* which is quoted in this current work, as well as in his other sixty books and writings, preceding and post illumination.

Another quote of Murry which hints at a broadened perspective, and which displays a newly engendered insight into the mind and writings of others, reads, "Poetry was no longer a strange and irrelevant loveliness in a chaotic world; it was a necessary and consummate flowering on the great tree of Life; it was *the* immanent purpose of the universe made vocal."

Once again, Murry speaks of himself as a thinker, and that "to reduce a surmise of this kind to any degree of intellectual clarity" was the work of years. However, he could apply it to the particular case of Keats. He also believed that he could apply it to Shakespeare... In studying Keats, Murry also realized, "The intimate connection between the pure mystical and the pure poetic experience was manifest." (Endnotes 27, 28)

Murry sought to painstakingly analyze the mystical experience, "in the attempt to separate the truth and value of that experience from whatever elements of illusion, or potential illusion, it might contain." (Endnote 29) He further states of Part II, "It is an attempt to connect, to expand, to order, and above all to criticize, all that is implicit in this piece of autobiography, and to separate out from it the elements of dependable verity from the elements of illusion it may contain."

He writes that he imposed "the most stringent intellectual criticism upon" himself. He has dedicated himself to truth: therein, he states "...the number of men is steadily increasing for whom whatever Faith they may achieve must be coherent with whatever Truth they know. To them this book is addressed." (Endnotes 30, 31) Murry was an intellectual, intellectualized.

**Loss of the Fear of Death**

To the best of my knowledge, Murry spoke little to nothing of the loss of the fear of death. Although after illumination and after his own experience had faded, he made one essential statement. He asserted that after reading of those great men, he would feel a serene illumination. He felt the feeling was expressed in "Lord, now lettest thou thy servant depart in peace, for mine eyes have seen my salvation." (Endnote 32)

**Loss of the Sense of Sin**

After illumination, in the initial stages of attempting to sort out his emotions, along with what he came to believe was a form of illusion, Murry stated, "I veritably believed that some sort of endorsement by the Universe was guaranteed to all my doings, and that I could do no wrong." (Endnote 33) He also stated, "I was quite incapable of analyzing the causes of this success and I naively took it as a confirmation of my own fundamental rightness."

In the latter half of *God*, Murry elaborated on the sense of illusion. Precisely how the concept of *fundamental rightness*, or of possible illusion, integrates the question of "Is there no conscience or is there no sin," and how both the conscience and the loss of the sense of sin hark back to fundamental rightness, cannot be answered currently. Should the reader be interested in pursuing this conundrum further, perhaps clues may be found in Murry's writings, subsequent to 1923.

### Suddenness, Instantaneousness, of the Awakening

Once again, I refer to Murry's statement of the moment of the mystical experience, "And I became aware of myself as a little island against whose slender shores a cold, dark, boundless ocean lapped devouring. Somehow in that moment..."

### Previous Character of the Man—Intellectual, Moral, and Physical; Prior to Illumination

Murry, the intellectual, has already been proven via his historical reputation and successes prior to illumination.

Before illumination, his tutor had called him inhuman. This description, which Murry provides showing the nature of his character prior to illumination, does not appear to meet the criteria for "previous moral character" set forth by Bucke. However, the dire circumstances from his youth onward, may have hampered, or overshadowed what, under normal circumstances, would have been considered a grand moral character.

It could not have been more apparent, however, that after the spiritual experience, he vaulted to unknown heights. Concurrent with illumination, according to Murry's own words, "The 'presence' of Katherine Mansfield was of the same order as the 'presence' which filled the room and me. In so far as the 'presence' was connected with her it had a moral quality, or a moral effect: I was immediately and deeply convinced that 'all was well with her.'" (Endnote 34) The newly endowed moral influence, even if this conclusion were based solely upon the virtue of the above affirmation, witnesses the acquisition of a greater moral stance.

I know little of his physical condition prior to illumination. Still, as indicated in the following, he lived the anticipated life-term as projected by Bucke. (See Age of Illumination, below.)

## Age of Illumination

Murry was born on August 6, 1889, and died on March 12, 1957. He succeeded to the spiritual experience in February 1923, making him nearly age 34. Of those persons identified in Bucke's book, fourteen of those thirty-four, whose age of illumination was known, entered illumination prior to age thirty four. Bucke believed that, for those suited, illumination arrives at about the height of maturity, or about the midpoint of life. Murry lived to be 68, precisely double the 34 years.

***

One more word: in belief, and through stark or blind determination in grief-born desperation, both Murry and I sought out the unknown. We each loved and unexpectedly lost a dear loved one through death. We lost an earthly love. Yet in the furthermost recesses of our being we must have understood that the love, the earthly love, a love conjoined by man—but inherent of, united, with the Eternal—exists eternally!

We must have known that our loved one, freed from earthy encumbrances, had survived in full virtuous fashion in some untold unknown manner, with what I call the Love Eternal. We must have known that *each* life, each love, continues to *live*, to thrive: each coexists, conjoined with the Eternal.

In our sheer overburdening sorrow, pure logic set itself aside. We each followed our instinct, the activity of which seemed normal at the time. We were determined to fling all discretion

## A Tiny But Radiant Light

aside in our adamant resolution to restore our being, or to *locate* our loved one. In doing so, all else, all material objects, and personal attributes and possessions became nil, or of no serious consequence. Stark pure intent was prevalent and would not yield nor dissolve.

Therein, with the attendance of the all-knowing-supreme, stood the potential to reconnect *on the level of our love*: each of us was successful, although in differing degrees, and with varying effects. At a minimum, I believe that Murry entered directly into an imperfect instance of illumination, and quite possibly into a greater instance of illumination. Initially, in the determined attempt to reconnect with my mother, I believe that I was launched on a dedicated spiritual pathway; and, years later, to the entryway into what I have termed for myself as embrightenment.

You see dear soul, with the determination, with the belief, with the explicit faith, the Eternal took control and brought us each to our purposed destination, the appropriate stance for each of us, at that time of our life.

\*\*\*

Murry concluded that the ultimate effects, and, perhaps, purpose, of the mystical experience is to merge the knowledge of the Mind with the feelings of the Heart declaring a new unified man, a new person. Frequently in this material life these appear to be contrary, or contradictory.

I agree with Murry's assertion: the mystical experience does merge the knowledge of the Mind with the feelings of the Heart. *While I am at-one-with* the Calm, I feel a unification, a peacefulness. Most important, there is a uniting of the intellect and the emotions: I am *at one*. There appears to be no contradiction in my being. This is true when the effects of the mystical experience are apparent—while vibrant—living within the individual. Along with each of the other named attributes, this coherence, this harmony, will also diminish over time leaving it, and the bulk of the gifts, to the active memory. Nevertheless, a contented mellowness apparently never leaves.

Murry learned "that a spiritual progress is possible to man, by which out of the discordant elements of his being—the desire of the Heart and the knowledge of the Mind—a harmony is created. This harmony was a new kind of being, and it had been called by Jesus and Eckhart and Keats, the Soul. This Soul was at once a new condition of the total human being and a faculty of knowledge." (Endnote 35) "A new kind of consciousness was created in them. Mind and Heart, which had been irreconcilable enemies, became united in the Soul, which loved what it knew." (Endnote 36)

The analytical Part II of *God*, is complex and involved, posing *the possibility of a reconciliation between Science and Religion*. Murry's final words, written after the completion of the entire book, (Endnote 37) were "…more…was required…" He "went on to describe the actual writing of the book…" There is no productive way to summarize Murry's final words except to quote the final sentence: "The variation must have emerged before it can know itself."

Focus on Murry's final sentence, "The variation must have emerged before it can know itself." Murry's sentence renders additional light to the understanding. As a person blind bears not the foundation with which to comprehend, nor to judge light and color. So, too, it is impossible to accurately render to the reader the true nature of the mystical experience, and of what Murry calls its "mystical certainty," to one who may be "listening" from the *outside* in. Murry says "…he (the writer) is conscious that his attempt to formulate and to communicate it in religious or poetical terms are always in some sense metaphorical." (Endnotes 38, 39)

Murry's final analysis, ensconced in the latter portion of his work, depending on the individual's expectation or viewpoint, may be extraordinarily worth assimilating. His thought is not difficult to follow, though at certain junctures, according to the "Heart"—at least according to this heart—some of his assertions and conclusions are a challenge to an understanding heart. Murry was an enlightened man. He was remarkable and brilliant.

To understand his conclusions properly one definitely must read *God* in its entirety in Murry's own words, following his own extensive thought process. The majority of the latter part of *God* does not generally rest within the purview of this current narrative.

## CHAPTER XI
## Endnotes

Endnote 1
Murry, J. Middleton, *God*, New York and London, *Harper & Brothers Publishers*, 1929.

Endnote 2
Author unknown: A newspaper clipping of unknown origin was pasted into my copy of Murry's *God*, which contained the following sentence written about Murry, "The powerful spiritual experience which followed this realization brought in its wake a feeling of 'serene illumination.'"
After illumination, and after his own experience had grown dim, when rereading the great lives of two men, Murry reported that as he "relived the exaltations and re-endured the agonies of those men, the extraordinary feeling of serene illumination would flood my soul..." Ibid., § 13, p 65.

Endnote 3
Ibid., *Autobiography*, § 2, p 5.

Endnote 4
Murry, J. Middleton, *God*, New York and London, *Harper & Brothers Publishers*, 1929, *Autobiography*, § 7, pp 26-31. Murry's firsthand report of his spiritual experience and its subsequent analysis is not only illuminating, but bears a tremendous advantage to seek out and read.

Endnote 5
In a separate location, appearing after the initiation of a detailed consideration of the mystical experience and its aftereffects, Murry hones in on the subject of the conflict, or opposition, between the conclusions of the Mind with its thought (intellectual man), and the desires of the Heart with its emotion (instinctive man). He states of the

mystical experience: "Then comes the *explosion* (Italics by this writer). There is a sudden and unique experience of the kind which I have attempted to describe in the first section of this book. It is an immediate experience of an all-pervading Unity." Ibid.,*Mysticism and After*, § 2-3, p 130-132; § 8, p 153; § 12, p 172.

Another essential statement by Murry reads: "Suddenly, there is a solution of the insoluble. There is created within the subject a new kind of consciousness, in which emotion and thought, previously in absolute opposition, become one and indistinguishable. The subject experiences a new unity, in which the previously separated Heart and Mind are one. And this unity is not distinct from the Universe, but an inseparable part of it. At one and the same moment, the subject experiences himself as a unity, and this unity of himself as part of an all-pervading Unity." Ibid., § 8, p 136.

Endnote 6

A curious aside: Murry's work became known under striking circumstances. Approximately seven years after the mystical evening of 1991, I accidently *Stumbled* across his book at a sale at the local public library. To the self-conscious mind, even then, the circumstance appeared to be greater than a mere coincidence.

A bare few weeks prior to the discovery of the book, in passing, I overheard one solitary sentence of a conversation between a restaurant patron and his waitress. He said, "You should read the book, *God*." Alerted and keenly interested, I set it firmly in mind to acquire the book. However, I did not. After overhearing the snippet of conversation, and shortly thereafter *inadvertently* finding the book, I now postulate that this *happenstance* was unmistakably by design; it was meant to be.

Endnote 7

Possibly, this is the time for a few merely personal remarks before delving further into similarities: I feel compelled to reiterate all that has been brought into the earthy atmosphere by the Living Light which dwells within, and which *toils* with-under the charter of the poetry. At long last after eight years of retirement; serious illness in the immediate family; the accidental death of a beloved father; a daughter confident in her own life; a great grandson beginning to attend school full-time, I am prompted to use my time to complete what appears to be life's-end purpose.

This prompting alone justifies the Sturm und Drang over this manuscript and its fervent intent to assure its absolute accuracy despite the travail of ineffectual language. At a minimum, to my active mind, the undertaking is to impart the direct knowledge, in some coherent manner, of one person's mystical experience in the twentieth century. In supposition, this endeavor may invite a greater curiosity to entice or to encourage another to broaden or to strengthen their personal spiritual journey, yet, to persist in the manner that each individual person deems fit.

Life bears hope and death bears hope. Life seems at times to be such a rugged road to travel; nonetheless, such a lovely adventurous exciting road to travel. In the early and even in the latter years of my search, I relied heavily on information provided by others to uplift and nudge me forward. Perhaps, that alone makes this attempt at writing acceptable.

Let us face it. No one can merely "think this up." It simply would not be worth their effort or the multitude of years that it would take. And, I am too old to need any potential profit. I do not believe there is an ulterior motive other than the habitual prodding from within. These four paragraphs were a huge sidestep, yet this feeling persists at this juncture, so it is released and written.

Endnote 8
Murry, J. Middleton, *God*, New York and London, *Harper & Brothers Publishers*, 1929, Part I, *Autobiography*, § 6, pp 24-26; § 7, pp 26-31.

Endnote 9
Ibid., *Autobiography*, § 13, p 63: *Mysticism and After*, § 1, p 131.

Endnote 10
Alone in the Avion, in Batesville, Arkansas, September 21, 2007, seventeen years after the mystical experience, while rereading *God*, my heart was glowing with joy. Unforeseen, the mood and emotion of the evening and moment of July 1991 returned and overcame me in its intensity.

Pencil in hand, in remembrance in spontaneity, I wrote: "I was verging on the twilight and I "knew" already, still did not know that I knew. Sound strange? Not in the least. The dawning was glowing, yet comprehension was lagging until the bright flame of day burst forth from within swiftly carried by the thunderous raging swiftly rushing of winds striking me, igniting and flashing upward, then outward and downward in a ravenous intimate slowly traveling fury. Then calm. The storm had passed and left its bountiful benefits, immediately to grow and prosper. The ground sanctified by the glorious Calm, nurtured by the Love, and watered by my tears.

Endnote 11
  Ibid., *The New Man*, § 4, p 94.

Endnote 12
  Murry received a defaming letter from a friend. The friend had heard that Murry was writing about the life of Jesus, which meant that he felt that he understood Jesus, Murry had to admit, at least to himself, that a method such as his does involve placing oneself momentarily on a level with great men.
  Murry wrote, "I had begun to believe that, at least in part, I understood Jesus. That was the reason why I was drawn to write about him: I wished, if I could, to understand wholly what I believed I understood in part. But if the initial and partial understanding had been denied me nothing would have induced me to make the attempt. I was not then, and I am not now in myself aware of any presumption. I had been given an experience that enabled me to understand things that had been hidden from me for many years. A clue had been placed in my hands which it was my duty to follow where it led; and I was determined to follow it. A means of understanding had been granted to me, and I must use it. To refuse was to deny myself." *God, Autobiography*, § 11-12, pp 56-57.

Endnote 13
  Murry, J. Middleton, *God*, New York and London, *Harper & Brothers Publishers*, 1929, Autobiography, § 13, p 66.

Endnote 14
Murry, J. Middleton, *God*, New York and London, *Harper & Brothers Publishers*, 1929, *Autobiography*, § 12, p 57.
  While Murry labeled his experience, "An experience that enabled me to understand," Gautama says plainly, "*Arahatship* enables a man to comprehend by his own heart the hearts of other beings and of other men, to understand all minds, the passionate, the calm, the angry, the peaceable, the deluded, the wise, the concentrated, the ever varying, the lofty, the narrow, the sublime, the mean, the steadfast, the wavering,

the free, and the enslaved. (Akankheyya-Sutta, Translated from Pali by T.W. Rhys Davids, in Volume XI of 146.)

Endnote 15
Ibid., *Autobiography*, § 9, p 47.

Endnote 16
"Then comes the explosion. There is a sudden and unique experience of the kind which I have attempted to describe in the first section of this book. It is an immediate experience of an all-pervading unity." Ibid., *Mysticism and After*, § 2, p 132.

Endnote 17
Murry, J. Middleton, *God*, New York and London, *Harper & Brothers Publishers*, 1929, *Autobiography*, § 14, p 69.

Endnote 18
Ibid., *Mysticism and After*, § 1, p 126-127.

Endnote 19
Ibid., Autobiography, § 14, p 69.

Endnote 20
Ibid., § 8, p 34.

Endnote 21
THE UNSEEN HAND, A handbook of yoga way of life for self-realization, YOGI RAUSHAN NATH, Foreword by DR. KARAN SINGH, RAJIV PUBLICATIONS, NEW DELHI, June 1971. Distributors: Trimuri Publications, W-152, Greater Kailash-I, New Delhi-48. PRINTED BY: NEW INDIA PRESS, K-BLOCK, CONNAUGHT CIRCUS, NEW DELHI-1. AUTHOR'S NOTE, p XIV.

Endnote 22
Murry, J. Middleton, *God*, New York and London, *Harper & Brothers Publishers*, 1929, *Autobiography*, § 2, pp 6-9; § 3, pp 10-14.

Endnote 23
Perhaps, in part, his attitude was unduly influenced by the sudden death of his childhood friend, who he had been playing with when the lightning struck.

Endnote 24
Murry, J. Middleton, *God,* New York and London, *Harper & Brothers Publishers,* 1929, *Autobiography,* § 11, pp 53-54.

Endnote 25
Ibid., § 8, p 34.

Endnote 26
Murry quotes Meister Eckhart in his *Eternal Rebirth of the Soul* as containing "almost an exact description of my experience; and I shall not easily forget the shock of delighted recognition at certain of his words. After that rebirth, he says, 'the reborn soul is as the eye, which having gazed into the sun, thenceforward sees the sun in everything.' That beautiful phrase more nearly conveys the quality of vision during the days which followed my experience than any other words I know." Ibid., § 8, p 33.

Endnote 27
Murry, J. Middleton, *God,* New York and London, *Harper & Brothers Publishers,* 1929, *Autobiography,* § 11, pp 53-54.

Endnote 28
Ibid., § 10, p 52.

Endnote 29
Ibid., § 7, p 29.

Endnote 30
Ibid., § 7, p 33.

Endnote 31
Ibid., § 7, p 83.

Endnote 32
Ibid., § 13, p 65.

Endnote 33
Ibid., § 7, p 32.

Endnote 34
Ibid., § 7, p 31.

Endnote 35
Ibid., § 2, p 66.

Endnote 36
Ibid., § 14, p 68.

Endnote 37
Murry, J. Middleton, *God*, New York and London, *Harper & Brothers Publishers*, 1929, *Epilogue*, § 2, pp 343-344.

Endnote 38
Ibid., *Mysticism and After*, § 1, p 123.

Endnote 39
For a primary example of the aforesaid, consider the "winds." The winds range from the swiftly rushing or racing, thunderous, to the differing and diminished rhythm of wings sweeping or beating. The rhythm, which accompanies the winds, the poetry, or which accompanies the visions, may be described as pulsing, vibrating, humming, quivering, quavering, and on and on. The language bears no true counterpart to the "experience" experienced. It renders pure knowledge, which cannot be upbraided, but which cannot convey the precise concept of the wavering, or the emotion of the instantaneous recognition, a revelation, the effect of the intensity, and of the varying length of the lingering afterglow.

Language cannot describe the clarity of thought or the presence of the Presence. Reading only provides a semblance of the veracity of the experience. As the reader may become impatient with a writer when trying to describe something as elusive as a mystical experience or an emotion, the writer also becomes impatient with trying to describe sensations with their accompanying thought, or with the variance of overlap or interface each emotion or sensation may play with each other or with another similar in nature.

## CHAPTER XII

## WALT WHITMAN—Onset of Illumination, by Virtue of Association with Whitman

### Germination or Bud: The Tender Touch

    I have long since known, and now recognize wholly, that the rhythm living within Whitman's poetry, *Leaves of Grass*, builds up or compounds in a person's body over a shorter or prolonged period. Undoubtedly, the length of time is dependent upon the nature of the individual and the unique array of circumstances. The effect of the rhythm upon the physical has the capacity, in combination with other factors, to cause an ignition, an enkindling, a spontaneous bursting-forth or flare interiorly, such as a match striking flint to ignite flame.

    In the instance of this writer, it occurred within the head within the upper middle brain. Then the resultant pulsing affect traveled as described in *Thunderous Sound: the Enkindling*. Although, in Whitman's case, his poetry appears to indicate that it began in the region of the hips "... and gently turn'd over on me." And, it appears that the manifestation traveled "...and plunged your tongue to my bare-stript heart, and reach'd till you felt my beard, and reach'd till you held my feet..." (Endnote 1)

    Whitman adeptly recollects in an early poem, *Song of Myself*:
"*I believe in you my soul—the other I am must not abase itself
    to you;
And you must not be abased to the other.
Loafe with me on the grass—loose the stop from your throat
Not words, not music or rhyme I want—not custom or lecture,
    not even the best;*

## Margaret Mary Stender

*Only the lull I like, the hum of your valvéd voice.*
*I mind how once we lay, such a transparent summer morning;*
*(Endnote 2, 3)*
*How you settled your head athwart my hips, and gently turn'd*
  *over upon me,*
*And parted the shirt from my bosom-bone, and plunged your*
  *tongue to my bare-stript heart,*
*And reach'd till you felt my beard, and reach'd till you held*
  *my feet.*

*Swiftly arose and spread around me the peace and knowledge*
  *that pass all the argument of the earth;*
*And I know that the hand of God is the promise of my own,*
*(Endnote 4, 5)*
*And I know that the spirit of God is the brother of my own;*
*And that all the men ever born are also my brothers, and the*
  *Women my sisters and lovers;*
*And that the kelson of the creation is love;*

The illumination experience of Whitman, described in approximately twenty-one sentences, closely tallies the experience of those illumined others, as shown succinctly by Bucke. Certain elements also coincide with the case of John Middleton Murry. However, in one short selection from *Leaves of Grass*, Whitman effortlessly and mindfully describes his personal illumination experience. Herein are a few correlating comments:

**First, the Prelude to the Illumination Experience:** Whitman believes; "I believe in you my soul…"which means that he has a faithful determination. He secures a peaceful location; He loafs. He invites; "Loafe with me on the grass…" He values the lull, "the hum of your valved voice"; he proclaims a silent calm and rhythm.

**Second, the Moment of Illumination:** "You settled your head"; made yourself a home with me, my companion and mate. "and gently turn'd over upon me"; the ecstasy traveled. "…and plunged your tongue into my bare-strip heart." "You reached"; the ecstasy traveled upward to the beard and downward to the feet.

**Thereafter, the Immediate Aftereffect:** "Swiftly arose and spread around me the peace and knowledge that pass all the argument of the earth"; you imparted a powerful knowledge, a calm. He is aware that he is possessed of the unity: The individual is conjoined with the supreme, the finite with the infinite. He knows "that the hand of God is the promise of my own." He knows "that the spirit of God is the brother of my own."

The object of this brief section is to, once again, reiterate and commend the rhythm in Whitman's poetry, to applaud the man himself: to reinforce the contention that under the right circumstance, the rhythm ensconced in the poetry has the potential to engender a condition which may cause one to unexpectedly enter into the state of illumination.

As previously stated, consistent with my personal experience, if Whitman's *Leaves of Grass* is read heartily over an extended period, illumination, at least in twilight, is inevitable. In Bucke's judgment, personal interaction with Whitman also bears the potential for illumination. His friends and acquaintances deeply valued Whitman's poetry as well as treasured his friendship.

Whitman, himself, believed that illumination would come to his longtime friend, Horace Traubel. He did not seem surprised upon hearing of Traubel's "run of good luck"; Whitman remarked, "I knew it would come to you." (Endnote 6)

*Ever Faithful*, a poem addressed to the Love Eternal, with an appreciative reference to Whitman, and to his influence, by virtue of the generation of a form of the rhythm, appears in the Appendix. Rhythm cracks open the door to a myriad of mystical experience; *From Whooshing Storms of Sea to Bearing Life and Calm*—a lengthy poem mentioning Whitman, which acknowledges the rhythm, also appears in the Appendix.

# Margaret Mary Stender

## Selection from *So Go As Thou Are!*

*"O Prophet heavenly, extract from the poetry,*
*    the few, the clues buried—still, shining deep within,*
*And read, especially read, Walt Whitman's 'Leaves'*
*    having written underneath—beneath the lines*
*        —the leaves,*
*Having given of his efforts, of his time to encourage folk.*
*    Though, it cannot be said for certain,*
*Where and when in his experience—his body it began,*
*    it appears to be beneath his heart—though, too,*
*It was within his head in its intensity, in its spread*
*    —in light, so few approach.*
*"And still, O Prophet heavenly,*
*    the humanity in me speaks for answers,*
*As with answers given, knowledge of the central core,*
*    the chastity, the purity, the interaction physically,*
*Its effects and attributes freely, precisely*
*    —pricelessly given."*
*        8/25/1995 TGS*

## CHAPTER XII
## Endnotes

Endnote 1
*Leaves of Grass,* by Walt Whitman, including a facsimile autobiography variorum readings of the poems and a department of Gathered Leaves, Toronto, The Musson Book Co., Limited, Copyright, 1900, by David McKay, Press of Sherman & Co., Philadelphia, *Walt Whitman*, First published in 1855, Part 5, p 34-35.
Note: The poem *Walt Whitman* was later retitled, *Song of Myself.*
The poem *Poets to Come* is found on page 195. (Walt Whitman's poem *Song of Myself* may also be found in the public domain on the Internet.)

Endnote 2
Ibid., "once" added in 1860.

Endnote 3
Ibid., "how" added in 1860.

Endnote 4
Ibid., 1855 reads "elderhand of my own."

Endnote 5
Ibid., 1855 reads "eldest brother."

Endnote 6
Bucke, Richard Maurice, M.D., *Cosmic Consciousness, A Study in the Evolution of the Human Mind*, with an Introduction by George Moreby Acklom, New York, E. P. DUTTON AND COMPANY, INC., Publishers: Introduction is dated New York City, February 25, 1946. 14th Edition, 1948, Chapter 33, Horace Traubel, p 346.

Margaret Mary Stender

## CHAPTER XIII

## ELSA BARKER—Written Through the Hand of... 1914

After this entire composition is in large part complete, I am backtracking and inserting an unplanned section to this book. In August 2009, my Batesville, Arkansas friend, Samm, absolutely insisted that I read a book that to him was vitally potent and inspiring. After a fine dinner together at his favorite Chinese Restaurant, he, a man just days away from his 85th birthday, insisted that I wait in the car while he hobbled down an uneven incline to his home. Relying heavily on his cane to support the horrendous endeavor, he went blithely into his home to retrieve *Letters from a Living Dead Man.* (Endnote 1) How little did Samm know that he was giving me one expediency so akin to my own.

Glued to the inside of the front book cover was a copy of what appeared to be a sheet of an official notepad containing the heading MITCHELL KENNERLEY (Then appeared a symbol, MK, within a circle) PUBLISHER NEW YORK. The right-hand side of the paper was slightly ragged and cut away, apparently to make it fit within the size of the book cover. With irregular indentations, the upper portion of the sheet read:

FOURTH LARGE EDITION
LETTERS FROM A
LIVING DEAD MAN
WRITTEN DOWN BY ELSA BARKER

## A Tiny But Radiant Light

The critical middle section, handwritten and signed by Elsa Barker, read:

> Dear Mr. Kennerley: I give you my personal assurance, unqualified by any reservation whatever, that the experiences recorded in this book occurred precisely as I have explained in the Introduction. Elsa Barker

The writer, Elsa Barker, described that, "One night last year in Paris I was strongly impelled to take up a pencil and write, though what I was to write about I had no idea. Yielding to the impulse, my hand was seized as if from the outside, and a remarkable message of a personal nature came, followed by the signature 'X.'" (Endnote 2) Later Barker was informed by a friend that a mutual friend, Judge David Patterson Hatch, was known as "X." Four years of automatic writing from *a Living Dead Man* had begun.

Because of Samm's enthusiasm, I began to read in earnest that very night. Although, I must admit that I laid the book aside the following day. As enlightening and fascinating as it was, it was slightly out of sync with what I wished to read at the time. The following day, feeling guilty, out of concern for returning the book before I had to return to my home in Michigan, and especially out of respect for his excellent judgment, I once again secured a comfortable chair and began to read. (An outline of Samm's mystical experience appears in the Appendix.)

And, lo, oh blessed, when I came to the chapter titled *LETTER XXXV, The Beautiful Being*, my heart began to swell and hum in joyous harmonious accord. At about the point of "Come out and play with me in the daisy fields of space..." I perceived the Presence! Instantly, I literally recognized the presence of the state of illumination or enlightenment *indwelling* the originator while penning, or dictating, this poem. I also felt the calming affects within my own being.

A glimpse of the cosmic sense soared-spontaneous in-sweeping me with its all-encompassing all-powerful fervor. As I write this, I still tingle in joyous resonance with peace and love. I glow. It is as if there is the recognition of oneself to oneself.

It was the language of this letter that first drew my attention, stirred my desire, and reawakened my memory. Initially the chapter was merely being read as one would read any normal interesting document; that is until I came to the words, "I seemed to be reclining upon a moonbeam, and ecstasy filled my heart." Upon reading those words, my mind made one gigantic quantum leap and overtly questioned, "I wonder if he knows what 'ecstasy' really means?"

Therein, immediately, I began to take acute interest in gleaning the entirety of the message. Within a few seconds, amazed, I realized that the *writer* undeniably does, indeed, comprehend what the word ecstasy means, "that state of etheric joy." It was clear that the entity, on the other side of the veil, writing through the hand of Elsa Barker, possessed direct knowledge of the illumination experience and of the ecstasy by virtue of a similar manifestation of the experience, and to an exceptionally predominant degree.

Although *it* was being called by another title, namely, the Beautiful Being, it was unquestionably what I recognize as cosmic consciousness, or to one in possession of the cosmic sense.

***

The first part of LETTER XXXV, *The Beautiful Being*, describes and confirms the illumination experience; an experience that if dissected will nearly precisely meet the criterion for illumination as defined by Richard Maurice Bucke. In fact, the LETTER is immeasurably significant as it continues with, "I must have been enjoying a foretaste of that paradoxical state which the wise ones of the East call Nirvana."

It is of great value to secure the book and to thoughtfully read the paragraph beginning with "One night I seemed to be reclining upon a moonbeam..." The author of the Letter took the *time* to deliberately and accurately describe the prelude to illumination: the description is straightforward and is abundantly manifest to every person possessing the slightest inclination of the illumination experience.

(The sentence predictably revived the light of my tiny candle.)

Reader, while savoring the words quoted below, pay particular attention to the gentleness of tone, the elegance of thought. Dwell on and absorb the content word by word, sentence by sentence. Affirmatively attempt to reduce any tension within the body. Then attempt to acquire, or to recognize, the feeling generated in both the body and the mind by the poetic cadence of the words. (Endnote 3)

Read, this, the first part of LETTER XXXV, *The Beautiful Being*, slowly several times if necessary. Solemnly begin to focus with, "Shall I tell you of one whom I call the Beautiful Being?" You shall hear the "heart" speak frankly and sincerely: (Endnote 4) The paragraph begins with: "Yes, I have seen angels, if by angels you mean spiritual beings who have never dwelt as men upon the earth."

> Yes, I have seen angels, if by angels you mean spiritual beings who have never dwelt as men upon the earth.
>
> As a man is to a rock, so is an angel to a man in vividness of life. If we ever experience that state of etheric joy, we have lost it through long association with matter. Can we ever regain it? (Endnote 5) Perhaps. The event is in our hand.
>
> Shall I tell you of one whom I call the Beautiful Being? If it has a name in heaven, I have not heard it. Is the Beautiful Being man or woman? Sometimes it seems to be one, sometimes the other. There is a mystery here which I cannot fathom.
>
> One night I seemed to be reclining upon a moonbeam, which means that the poet which dwells in all men was awake in me. I seemed to be reclining upon a moonbeam, and ecstasy filled my heart. For the moment I had escaped the clutches

of Time and was living in that etheric quietude which is merely the activity of rapture raised to the last degree. I must have been enjoying a foretaste of that paradoxical state which the wise ones of the East call Nirvana.

I was vividly conscious of the moonbeam and of myself, and *in* myself seemed to be everything else in the universe. It was the nearest I ever came to a realization of that supreme declaration, *"I am."*

The past and the future seemed equally present in the moment. Had a voice whispered that it was yesterday, I should have acquiesced in the assertion; had I been told that it was a million years hence, I should have been also assentive. But whether it was really yesterday or a million years hence mattered not in the least. Perhaps the Beautiful Being only comes to those for whom the moment and eternity are one. I heard a voice say: "Brother, it is I."

There was no question in my mind as to who had spoken. "It is I" can only be uttered in such a voice by one whose individuality is so vast as to be almost universal, one who has dipped in the ocean of the All, yet who knows the minute by reason of its own inclusiveness.

Standing before me was the Beautiful Being, radiant in its own light. Had it been less lovely I might have gasped with wonder; but the very perfection of its form and presence diffused an atmosphere of calm. I marveled not, because the state of my consciousness *was* marvel. I was lifted so far above the commonplace that I had no standard by which to measure the experience of that moment.

Imagine youth immortalized, the fleeting made eternal. Imagine the bloom of a child's face and the eyes of the ages of knowledge. Imagine the brilliancy of a thousand lives concentrated in those eyes, and the smile upon the lips of a love so pure that it asks no answering love from those it smiles upon.

But the language of earth cannot describe the unearthly, nor could the understanding of man grasp in a moment those joys which the Beautiful Being revealed to me in that hour of supreme life. For the possibilities of existence have been widened for me. The meanings of the soul have deepened. Those who behold the Beautiful Being are never the same again as they were before. They may forget for a time, and lose in the business loving the magic of that presence; but whenever they do remember, they are caught up again on the winds of the former rapture.

It may happen to one who is living upon the earth; it may happen to one in the spaces between the stars; but the experience must be the same when it comes to all; for only to one in the state in which it dwells could the Beautiful Being reveal itself at all. (Endnote 6, 7)

One astounding inordinately enlightening thought, expressed in the first part of LETTER XXXV, *The Beautiful Being,* strikes a hierarchical position in one's conscious mind, strikes strangely and penetrates deeply, "It may happen to one who is living upon the earth; it may happen to one in the spaces between the stars; but the experience must be the same when it comes to all; for only to one in the state in which it dwells could the Beautiful Being reveal itself at all." This sentence alone will stand the test of *time*: it distinguishes the *mind* of the writer. It testifies to the state of illumination. It testifies to the fact of illumination.

Since according to Elsa Barker, this letter is dictated by a man on the other side of the veil, the above referenced sentence declares conclusively that the illumination/enlightenment experience may occur here in the material or natural world and may also occur subsequent to the boundary of so-called death, "in the spaces between the stars." It also implies that in this instance the Beautiful Being—or, perhaps, the Beautiful State of Consciousness (Endnote 8)—may have been first glimpsed, and became a supreme reality, a framework of the dictating entity's spiritual knowledge and *growth*, only after the earthly death! (Endnote 9)

But it is not necessarily true that this Being or this State—in this instance—may have first been glimpsed by the writer only after the earthly death. Take note of the following indication of an earthly knowledge "...nor could the understanding of man grasp" and "that hour of supreme life." These references decidedly portend to the "man" and plainly also suggest a knowledge—"meanings of the soul"—of an experience having occurred during the duration of the human lifetime.

They, the person or being, after encountering the Beautiful Being, "are never the same again as they were before."

It may be prudent to reread the above beginning with:

> But the language of earth cannot describe the unearthly, nor could the understanding of man grasp in a moment those joys which the Beautiful Being revealed to me in that hour of supreme life. For the possibilities of existence have been widened for me. The meanings of the soul have deepened. Those who behold the Beautiful Being are never the same again as they were before. They may forget for a time, and lose in the business loving the magic of that presence, but whenever they do remember, they are caught up again on the winds of the former rapture.

The concept that the cosmic sense may come to one after death is momentous. It is profound! This knowledge could propel a flaring flaming joy throughout the physical world of mankind,

## A Tiny But Radiant Light

and that in spite of any hefty temporal earthly woes. The concept of the Beautiful Being or Beautiful State of Consciousness augments knowledge and, to my mind, negates nothing.

The second portion of LETTER XXXV consists of the *Song of the Beautiful Being*: it speaks of the illustrious Joy:

> *A SONG OF THE BEAUTIFUL BEING*
> *(Endnote 10)*
>
> *When you hear a rustling in the air, listen again: there may be something there.*
>
> *When you feel a warmth mysterious and lovely in the heart, there may be something there, something sent to you from a warm and lovely source.*
>
> *When a joy unknown fills your being, and your soul goes out, out...toward some loved mystery, you know not where, know that the mystery itself is reaching toward you with warm and loving, though invisible, arms.*
>
> *We who live in the invisible are not invisible to each other.*
>
> *There are tender colors here and exquisite forms, and the eye gloats on beauty never seen upon the earth.*
>
> *Oh, the joy of simple life—to be, and to sing in your soul all day as the bird sings to its mate!*
>
> *For you are singing to your mate whenever your soul sings.*
>
> *Did you fancy it was only the springtime that thrilled you and moved you to listen to the rustling of wings?*

## Margaret Mary Stender

*The springtime of the heart is all time, and the autumn
    may never come.*

*Listen! When the lark sings, he sings to you. When
    the waters sing, they sing to you.*

*And as your heart rejoices, there is always another heart
    somewhere that responds and the soul of the listening heavens grows glad with the mother joy.*

*I am glad to be here, I am glad to be there. There is
    beauty wherever I go.*

*Can you guess the reason, children of earth?*

*Come out and play with me in the daisy fields of space.
    I will wait for you at the corner where the four
    winds meet.*

*You will not lose your way, if you follow the gleam at
    the end of the garden of hope.*

*There is music also beyond the roar of the earth as it
    swishes through space:*

*There is music in keys unknown to the duller ears of
    the earth, and harmonies whose chords are souls
Attuned to each other.*

*Listen. ...Do you hear them?
    Oh, the ears are made for hearing, and the eyes are
    made for seeing, and the heart is made for loving!*

*The hours go by and leave no mark, and the years are
    as sylphs that dance on the air and leave no footprints, and the centuries march solemn and slow.*

*But we smile, for joy is also in the solemn tread of the
    centuries.*

## A Tiny But Radiant Light

*Joy, joy everywhere. It is for you and for me, and for you as much as for me.*

*Will you meet me out where the four winds meet? (Endnote 11)*

In LETTER XXXVII, *Where Time is Not,* pp 187-194, one finds a reference, by the writer of these letters, which states that he "...felt a yearning for beauty, which is a synonym for heaven." "It was so beautiful" that it lent a charm which was over him still at time of the writing to Barker. (Endnote 12) "...a softly diffused light" akin to "a heaven lighted by a thousand suns," but this heaven was not like that. "The light...was softer than moonlight, though clearer. Perhaps the light of the sun would shine as softly if seen through many veils of alabaster. Yet this light seemed to come from nowhere. It simply was."

He realized that he "was in one of the fairest heavens, but he was alone there. Then, standing before him was the Beautiful Being. It smiled and said to him: "He who is sadly conscious of his solitude is no longer in heaven." The writer of these letters questioned, "Is this the particular heaven where you dwell?" The Beautiful Being answered. "I am one of the voluntary wanderers, who find the charm of home in every heavenly or earthly place." The writer of these letters responds "So you sometimes visit earth?"

Now, we hark back to the mystery of the sentence: "It may happen to one who is living upon the earth; it may happen to one in the spaces between the stars." This statement, "So you sometimes visit earth?" appears to positively indicate that the writer of these letters became *familiar* with the Beautiful Being, or beautiful state of consciousness, only after the earthly death.

He seemed surprised at the thought of the Beautiful Being finding "the charm of home in every heavenly or earthly place." The mere thought that the Beautiful Being could have come to him after the earthly death warms the heart and lightens the burden of earthly woes.

## Margaret Mary Stender

The Beautiful Being further reports that "the earth is one of my playgrounds, (Endnote 13) I sing to the children of earth sometimes; and when I sing to the poets, they believe that their muse is with them. Here is a song which I sang one night to a soul which dwells among men:

> *"My sister, I am often with you when you realise it not.*
>
> *For me a poet soul is a well of water in whose deeps I can see myself reflected.*
>
> *I live in a glamour of light and colour, which you mortal poets vainly try to express in magic words.*
>
> *I am in the sunset and in the star; I watched the moon grow old and you grow young.*
>
> *In childhood you sought for me in the swiftly moving cloud; in maturity you fancied you had caught me in the gleam of a lover's eye; but I am the eluder of men.*
>
> *I beckon and I fly, and the touch of my feet does not press down the heads of the blossoming daisies.*
>
> *You can find me and lose me again, for mortal cannot hold me.*
>
> *I am nearest to those who seek beauty—whether in thought or in form; I fly from those who seek to imprison me.*
>
> *You can come each day to the region where I dwell.*
>
> *Sometimes you will meet me, sometimes not; for my will is the wind's will, and I answer no beckoning finger:*
>
> *But when I beckon, the souls come flying from the four corners of heaven.*

## A Tiny But Radiant Light

*Your soul comes flying, too; for you are one of those I
   have called by the spell of my magic.*

*I have use for you, and you have meaning for me; I like
   to see your soul in its hours of dream and ecstasy.*

*Whenever one of my own dreams a dream of paradise,
   the light grows brighter for me, to whom all things
   are bright.*

*Oh, forget not the charm of the moment, forget not the
   lure of the mood!*

*For the mood is wiser than all the magi of earth, and
   the treasures of the moment are richer and rarer
   than the hoarded wealth of the ages.*

*The moment is real, while the age is only a delusion, a
   memory, and a shadow.*

*Be sure that each moment is all, and the moment is more
   than time.*

*Time carries an hour-glass, and his step is slow; his hair
   is white with the rime of years, and his scythe is
   dull with unwearied mowing;*

*But he never yet has caught the moment in its flight.
   He has grown old in casting nets for it.*

*Ah, the magic of life and of the endless combination of
   living things!*

*I was young when the sun was formed, and I shall be
   young when the moon falls dead in the arms of her
   daughter the earth.*

*Will you not be young with me? The dust is as nothing:
   the soul is all.*

### Margaret Mary Stender

*Like a crescent moon on the surface of a lake of water
is the moment of love's awakening;*

*Like a faded flower in the lap of the tired world is the
moment of love's death.*

*But there is love and Love, and the love of the light for
its radiance is the love of souls for each other.*

*There is no death where the inner light shines, irradiating the fields of the within—the beyond—the unattainable attainment.*

*You know where to find me."*

Sometime after stumbling upon (Endnote 14) the awe-inspiring cogency of the Beautiful Being—the most magnificent authorship—, I reread the initial chapters of *Letters from a Living Dead Man* to determine whether I had missed a prior reference, or hint, of the Beautiful Being. I had not. There are no references prior to LETTER XXXV. If one is drawn and their mood or their interest flares to follow up on other references to the Beautiful Being, there is one very fine chapter, LETTER XX, *The Man Who Found God,* (Endnote 15) and there are informative references to Lionel, as in LETTER XI, *The Boy—Lionel*, (Endnote 16) and the emitting of light.

LETTER XLI, *The Darling of the Unseen*, is a heart-welcoming chapter. The writer of these letters speaks of returning to this earth, and perhaps of retaining a memory. He speaks thus: "Perhaps, like most people, I shall have forgotten the details of my life before birth, and shall bring with me only vague yearning after the inexpressible, and the deep unalterable conviction that there are more things in earth and heaven than are dreamed of in the philosophy of the world's people. Perhaps if I almost remember but not quite, I shall be a poet in my next life." (Endnote 17)

## A Tiny But Radiant Light

An especial succeeding comment, thoroughly relevant to the current purview is, "But no one can be sad when the Beautiful Being is near. That is the charm of that marvelous entity: to be in its presence is to taste the joys of immortal life."

There are still references to the Beautiful Being subsequent to LETTER XXXV in Barker's work, and there is a small quantity of heartfelt poetry (which leaves one with a hunger for more), either inspired by or dictated by the Beautiful Being. The entire book is illuminating: and, in my opinion, is a marvel to all mankind.

\*\*\*

For another moment, let us refocus on the similarities, by the writer of these letters. Paragraphs ten and eleven in the first part of LETTER XXXVII, which speaks to the effluence of the Beautiful Being. Compare the excerpts of the narrative with the greatest of gifts which are identified herein, and which are endowed by virtue of the evening's mystical experience.

To recap—again—approximately eighteen years after the evening and moment continually referred to, it came to me that these gifts are called "the Five Proficiencies." These five were delineated in the section titled "Youth Within—*The Radiant Boy*," and are recognized as, "Knowledge Known, coexistent with Eternal Life; Calm—perceived as a light weight, but recognized as an intelligible Presence; the Love; and the Joy with its accompaniment, Youth." (Frequently, Knowledge Known, Eternal Life, immortality [as coexistent as they are] are not considered within the *five*; the Calm, Presence, Love, Joy and Youth are considered independently.)

The exact correlating excerpts spoken of by the writer of the LETTERS are: "radiant in its own light; diffused an atmosphere of calm; youth immortalised; the eyes of the ages of knowledge; a love so pure that it asks no answering love from those it smiles upon; those joys which the Beautiful Being revealed to me."

Specifically correlated, each is as follows:

**Knowledge—Knowledge Known, coexistent with Eternal Life**

> Speaking of the Beautiful Being: "...the eyes of the ages of knowledge."

**Calm—perceived as a light weight, but recognized as an intelligible Presence**

> Speaking of the Beautiful Being: "...the very perfection of its form and presence diffused an atmosphere of calm"

**Love—i.e. The Love**

> Speaking of the Beautiful Being: "...a love so pure that it asks no answering love from those it smiles upon"

**Joy and Youth—the Joy with its accompaniment, Youth.**

> Speaking of the Beautiful Being: "...those joys which the Beautiful Being revealed to me." And, "...youth immortalized, the fleeting made eternal"

Let us, once again, correlate the identical gifts delineated immediately above, and which are expounded herein, in the section *The New Life Living Within*, with references in the Barker *LETTERS*. The attendant poetry in *A Tiny but Radiant Light* was faithfully composed a decade prior to Barker's book of the *LETTERS* descending into these grateful arms.

Listen to the writer of the *LETTERS*, and the poetry ensconced therein, with the chimes, (Endnote 18) of an open heart! Look with a critical eye at the five primary gifts of distinction as they interrelate with pertinent selections in Barker's work. Open your heart to the profound.

Each of the gifts are listed first, Barker's work is quoted thereafter.

**Calm—The Silence Under the Sound**

> One night I seemed to be reclining upon a moonbeam, which means that the poet which dwells in all men was awake in me. I seemed to be reclining upon a moonbeam, and ecstasy filled my heart. For the moment I had escaped the clutches of Time and was living in that etheric quietude which is merely the activity of rapture raised to the last degree.

**Laudable Presence—The Bounty of Calm**

> Standing before me was the Beautiful Being, radiant in its own light. Had it been less lovely I might have gasped with wonder; but the very perfection of its form and presence diffused an atmosphere of calm. I marveled not, because the state of my consciousness *was* marvel. I was lifted so far above the commonplace that I had no standard by which to measure the experience of that moment.

**Love Eternal—O My Virgin Sophia…**

> Imagine the brilliancy of a thousand lives concentrated in those eyes, and the smile upon the lips of a love so pure that it asks no answering love from those it smiles upon. (Endnote 19)

**Riotous Bounteous Joy—Over-Joyousness Expounding Out**

> As a man is to a rock, so is an angel to a man in vividness of life. If we ever experience that state of etheric joy…

But the language of earth cannot describe the unearthly, nor could the understanding of man grasp in a moment those joys which the Beautiful Being revealed to me in that hour of supreme life.

You have met persons who seemed to radiate sunshine, whose very presence in a room made you happier. Have you asked yourself why? The true answer would be that by their lovely disposition they attracted round them a "cloud of witnesses" as to the joy and the beauty of life. ...Then, too, a joyous heart attracts joyous events. ...I have seen the Beautiful Being itself, more than once, hovering in ecstasy above an earthly creature who was happy. (Endnote 20)

> *The immortal loves to speak to the immortal*
> *in the mortal,*
> *and there is joy in calling to the joy which*
> *dozes in the heart of a soul of earth.*
> *When joy is awake, the soul is awake.* (Endnote 21)

Immediately following are individual lines from *A Song of the Beautiful Being*. (Endnote 22) Listen to the sound of the words, feel the rhythmic flow, perceive the mood they engender, and consider the words of Edward Carpenter briefly mentioned in a prior section, and tally the similarity; observe how they speak of the same flaming joy, bred by the eternal love.

> *When a joy unknown fills your being, and your soul*
> *goes out, out...toward some loved mystery, you*
> *know not where, know that the mystery itself is*
> *reaching toward you with warm and loving, though*
> *invisible, arms.*
> *Oh, the joy of simple life—to be, and to sing in your soul*
> *all day as the bird sings to its mate!*
>
> *For you are singing to your mate whenever your soul*
> *sings.*

## A Tiny But Radiant Light

*And as your heart rejoices, there is always another heart somewhere that responds and the soul of the listening heavens grows glad with the mother joy.*

*But we smile, for joy is also in the solemn tread of the centuries.*

*Joy, joy everywhere. It is for you and for me, and for you as much as for me.*

*Joy is coming back to the world some day, such joy as the world has never known. You will one day be glad to be alive again, and I mean all of you.* (Endnote 23)

### Youth Within—*The Radiant Boy*

Imagine youth immortalized, the fleeting made eternal. Imagine the bloom of a child's face and the eyes of the ages of knowledge.

But by my digressions one would say that I was in my second childhood. So I am—my second childhood in the so-called invisible. (Endnote 24)

**Other Pertinent Analogies:** Presented first are lines quoted from this current narrative. These are followed by a selection from LETTER XXXV, *The Beautiful Being*.

When writing of the golden glow, it frequently seems prudent to present it from the male point of view, though it is also known, by the finite conscious mind, that it should also be presented equally from the female point-of view, or from a neutral standpoint.

LETTER XXXV
Shall I tell you of one whom I call the Beautiful Being? If it has a name in heaven, I have not heard it. Is the Beautiful Being man or woman? Sometimes it seems to

be one, sometimes the other. There is a mystery here which I cannot fathom.

...a secondary or alternate level of consciousness, of awakefullness; one that is completely focused within its own selfhood, self-knowledge or self-awareness, without reference, or recourse, to the senses or any material thing normally manifest to the exterior senses; having access only to the knowledge pertinent to the episode at hand, and to no other; specifically entirely focused, actually absorbed in, or being one with the immediate—as it relates to thought about or concerning the immediate.

LETTER XXXV
The past and the future seemed equally present in the moment. Had a voice whispered that it was yesterday, I should have acquiesced in the assertion had I been told that it was a million years hence, I should have been also assentive. But whether it was really yesterday or a million years hence mattered not in the least. Perhaps the Beautiful Being only comes to those for whom the moment and eternity are one.

*\*\**

Each person mentioned herein has shared what to them is a sacred personal experience. Each person has expressed and described its graduating-interacting—to the finite mind, its near magical—effect, to the best of their enhanced, yet natural ability.

After a period of a sacred silence, each person feels the necessity—is impelled—to expound upon or to write; each lingers in its unrelenting mood. Each believes a tremendous life-enthralling benefit accompanies the mystical experience. Each believes that the knowledge gleaned must be passed forward; each proffers its advantages. Each recognizes there is a fertile grain, to perhaps *a hefty-ton*, of understanding which lends to the understanding of others and of their inspired writings. Each recognizes that the potential for illumination is inherent in every

## A Tiny But Radiant Light

individual.

Paraphrased, as Walt Whitman said, "Walt, you contain so much, why not let it out then?" And, as Edward Carpenter said, "Those and the like of those that have been my companions are with You also, and shall be to all time. I give you but a hint and a word of commendation. I open a door outwards." (Endnote 25)

Margaret Mary Stender

## CHAPTER XIII
## Endnotes

*Note: Letters from a Living Dead Man, War Letters from the Living Dead Man,* and *Last Letters of the Living Dead Man,* will be found in the entirety on the Internet.)

Endnote 1
*Letters from a Living Dead Man,* Written Down by Elsa Barker, With an Introduction, New York, Mitchell Kennerley, 1918, LETTER XXXV, *The Beautiful Being,* pp 168-172.

Endnote 2
The LETTERS were initially signed with the letter "X." They were written down by Elsa Barker, a purported communication from Judge David Patterson Hatch. The Introduction, page 8, reads: "He was a well-known lawyer nearly seventy years of age, a profound student of philosophy, a writer of books, a man whose pure ideals and enthusiasms were an inspiration to everyone who knew him."

LETTER XVII, *The Second Wife over There,* page 64, states: "Many people call me simply 'the Judge.'"

As a slight sidestep, in LETTER XXVII, *The Magic Ring,* page 119, is an essential statement regarding the purport of the book. It reads: "...I began to write soon after coming out (the change that is called death), and these letters are really the letters of a traveler in a strange country. They record his impressions, often his mistakes, sometimes perhaps his provincial prejudices..."

And again in LETTER XXXI, *A Problem in Celestial Mathematics,* page 142, "It is because I want to give to you, and possibly to others, a few scraps of knowledge which might be inaccessible to you by any other means, that I am coming back, and coming back, time after time, to talk with you."

And, yet, again in LETTER XXXII, *A Change in Focus,* page 149: "My object in writing these letters is primarily to convince a few

persons—to strengthen their certainty in the fact of immortality, or the survival of the soul after the bodily change which is called death."

In LETTER XXXIII, *Five Resolutions*, (the writer of these letters speaks of writing "through the hand of" Elsa Barker), page 154: "It means much to me this correspondence with earth. During my illness I used to wonder if I could come back sometimes, but I never imagined anything like this. I would not have supposed it possible to find any well-balanced and responsible person with daring enough to join me in the experiment." Namely the "experiment" being the communication between two planes of existence.

Endnote 3
If one were to read this entire selection a few times in a quiet and sincere manner, it should prove to generate a restful peaceful contentedness. It may have this mild titillating effect with merely one reading.

Endnote 4
*Letters from a Living Dead Man*, Written Down by Elsa Barker, With an Introduction, New York, Mitchell Kennerley, 1918, LETTER XXXV, *The Beautiful Being*, pp 167-172.

Endnote 5
*War Letters from the Living Dead Man*, Written Down by Elsa Barker, With an Introduction, New York, Mitchell Kennerley, 1915, LETTER XLI, *A Conclave of Masters*, states: "Some day the races of men will return to the love which they have now forgotten."

Endnote 6
*Letters from a Living Dead Man*, Written Down by Elsa Barker, With an Introduction, New York, Mitchell Kennerley, 1918, LETTER XXXV, *The Beautiful Being*, pp 167-172.

*A Song of the Beautiful Being*, pp 167-170, which constitutes the second half of LETTER XXXV, is stressed in this narrative in *Riotous Bounteous Joy*.)

Endnote 7
Ibid., LETTER XXXVIII, *Where Time is Not*, is another truly lovely chapter wherein the Beautiful Being states in part: "Here is a song which I sang one night to a soul which dwells among men." p 193. Thereafter, appears a song of the Beautiful Being.

LETTER LI, *The April of the World*, also a very commendable chapter, which reads in part: "The Beautiful Being lives in eternity, as we fancy that we live in time. Will you write down here another of that angel's chant?" p 273.

Endnote 8
It is of extreme interest that The Beautiful Being is always referred to as *it*: "Shall I tell you of one whom I call the Beautiful? If it has a name in heaven, I have not heard it."

Endnote 9
Another quote: "The Eternal position of all things independent of time, without beginning or end, operates everywhere. It works essentially where otherwise there is not hope. It accomplishes that which is deemed impossible. What appears beyond belief or hope emerges into truth after a wonderful fashion." COEHUM PHILOSOPHORUM by PARACELSUS, THE COELUM PHILOSOPHORIUM, OR BOOK OF VEXATIONS; By PHILIPPUS THEOPHRASTUS PARACELSUS, *God and Nature do Nothing in Vain*. 1493-1541

Endnote 10
*Letters from a Living Dead Man*, Written Down by Elsa Barker, With an Introduction, New York, Mitchell Kennerley, 1918, LETTER XXXV, *The Beautiful Being*, pp 168-172.

Endnote 11
Oh, reader, does this song remind you of the lovely poetry, of Edward Carpenter, located in *Riotous Bounteous Joy*?

Endnote 12
Then, and I marvel at this, he, the Judge, described a perfect description of the phenomenon of the golden glow! (See Balzac's description, pages 63-64)

Endnote 13
*Letters from a Living Dead Man*, Written Down by Elsa Barker, With an Introduction, New York, Mitchell Kennerley, 1918, LETTER XXXVIII, *Where Time is Not*, pp 191-194.

# A Tiny But Radiant Light

Endnote 14
A "greater than synchronicity" played a hefty role in the "stumbling upon."

Endnote 15
*Letters from a Living Dead Man*, Written Down by Elsa Barker, With an Introduction, New York, Mitchell Kennerley, 1918, LETTER XX, *The Man who found God*, pp 78-83.

Endnote 16
Ibid., *The Boy Lionel*, pp 35.

Endnote 17
Ibid., *The Darling of the Unseen*, pp 217.

Endnote 18
The reverberation.

Endnote 19
*Letters from a Living Dead Man*, Written Down by Elsa Barker, With an Introduction, New York, Mitchell Kennerley, 1918, LETTER XXXV, *The Beautiful Being*, p 169.

Endnote 20
Ibid., LETTER XLIII, *A Cloud of Witnesses*, pp 232-233.

Endnote 21
Ibid., LETTER LI, *The April of the World*, p 274.

Endnote 22
Ibid., LETTER XXXV, *The Beautiful Being*, pp 170-172.

Endnote 23
*Last Letters of the Living Dead Man*, LETTER XXI, *A Rambling Talk*. (There are also references to Joy in *War Letters from the Living Dead Man*.)

Endnote 24
*Letters from a Living Dead Man*, Written Down by Elsa Barker, With an Introduction, New York, Mitchell Kennerley, 1918, LETTER XLI, *The Darling of the Unseen*, p 217)

Endnote 25

*Towards Democracy*, Edward Carpenter. Complete Edition in Four Parts. Published by George Allen and Unwin Limited, at 40 Museum Street, London, W. C., And by S. Clarke Limited, at 41, Granby Row, Manchester, 1916, Part I, LIX, p 94.

A Tiny But Radiant Light

## CHAPTER XIV

## EVENING AND MOMENT COMMENTARY: THUNDEROUS SOUND—The Enkindling

A Few Stray, Yet, Perhaps, Pertinent Comments

Far Too Much Repetition, Yet, it Persists.
I have tried, in the best way I know, to make it clear.

Subsequent to the evening of the embrightenment, I was never able to wholly comprehend the reason why the momentum of the enkindling had just stopped when it did, just instantly stopped just below the arms and noticeably straight across the chest. This is as great a mystery, as the magnitude of the experience itself, and distresses and concerns me to this day.

Was it my "exterior" thought, at some juncture anticipating the immanent effect of the enkindling (expecting the vision of the fire, haze or pink cloud, when it reached the area of the heart), that caused the momentum, the intimate rapturous-pulsation, to halt, to vanish, to become nonexistent so abruptly? Was it this, the awakening of the normal, the *regular* consciousness, suppressing or supplanting the conjoined consciousness that instantly annihilated the traveling physical sensation? Based upon the immediacy, it is absolutely certain that it was.

As near as can be determined, the enkindling with its flare lasted a full fifteen seconds, or perhaps longer, during which time the awareness was focused and acute. In addition to the recognition of the exhibition of the startling sensation, I realized that a glorious phenomenal event was occurring. The astonished conscious mind adhered to every art and obstacle *along-the-route*.

The awareness analyzed the sounds, and the keen splaying pinnacle-point of manifestation and was amazed by its immaculate revelation, the sensation and amplification. Thunderstruck, enthralled, the conscientiousness followed as if led, as the event was happening; its mode of progress or travel—its extended time frame—and its rapturous effect throughout the upper body.

The consciousness was overcome with amazement and awe at the recognizable mode of expression, relished its magnified effect on the physical body, and was genuinely dumbfounded by the location of it! It is worth repeating again and again: the consciousness was perfectly engulfed by, and engrossed in, the "moment"—was completely at one with the experience—until the obliterating prohibited thought.

At no time during the duration of the experience did the conscious mind ever consider the outer—the external—world, its life, family, surroundings. It did, however, possess the express knowledge, and consider the illumination experience, explicitly, the life-flowing flaming-into-existence. Amazed, it also recognized the *distance* attained by the traveling of the rapture; the distance—above the head—which exceeded *what it knew to be its body*, the current physical body, (and, still, it did not consider the outward world).

At the present time, December 2007, there is a distinct contradiction in my own mind as to the "no lapse of time" referred to under *Thunderous Sound: The Enkindling*, specifically, the "…unique sympathetic rhythm—with no perceived interval of elapsed time between the simultaneous awakening with the breaking-forth through the darkness coexistent with the realization of the raging rhythmic winds, and when the winds arrived and struck." There appeared to be—and still appears to be a—*no lapse of time*. And yet, there was a registry to the mind of the severe surging winds breaking-forth through the darkness, *prior* to their actual strike and interaction with the body within the high-middle of the head. No amount of current analysis surmounts this apparent contradiction.

The *Winds*, less ferocious in subsequent years with their accompanying pulsation or quivering, occasionally represented themselves and sounded as wings with their fluttering. Never, however, after the evening did the winds or wings deliver the aforementioned rare moment. Although the subsequent *deliveries* were diminished in nature, they were never paltry in nature!

The physical experience differed wildly in several aspects and in one major aspect from any description that I had previously read concerning enlightenment (in this instance, termed embrightenment), or could have imagined; in effect, it never could have been anticipated. This solitary statement is, perhaps, truly, the understatement of the century. One could never conceive in advance of the express nature or mode of expression, specifically of the exact sensation, of the traveling of its momentum. Consider once again John Middleton Murry's striking statement of his mystical experience: "What happened then? If I could tell that, I should tell a secret indeed."

Edward Carpenter in *Towards Democracy*, (Endnote 1) written in poetic verse, also concurs and concurs with all the imbued emotion of the mystic. Carpenter's verse is spoken from the explicit overarching view of the newly acquired cosmic sense:

"For you, too, beyond this visible—through the gates of mortal passion and suffering—for the exhaled spirit,

For you, too, beyond this broken dream, this bitter waking in tears,

Something—how can I tell it?—which I have seen, which I might perhaps give you: and yet which I cannot give you, but in me waits also for you—O how long?

Something that I have promised. I give you the token faithfully when you recognize and return it shall you have that you desire."

One could intellectually anticipate the sudden 180-degree transformation in one's life, as a result of an experience of this nature. However, it is doubtful that one can conceive of the actual ennobling heftiness that the transformation grants and also *imposes*. In reality, the change constitutes an immediate substantive conjoining affirmative shift.

There exists a new informed perspective, a vital new outlook. What was "real" before becomes alive! Life Lives! There is a perception of an outward flow, a radiation of expanded wondrousness (the wonder of *it* all) feeling. Life "lives": and one knows, Life reigns and glows. There exists within the consciousness "a looking within" as well as "a looking without, *outside*." There exists a secret knowledge of the sacredness.

The transformation constitutes no conscious decision: One simply is the change. One has already perceptually changed with the enkindling, is a new creation, is virtually a new man, is one with the Unity, one with the harmony of the universe. He or she knows it!

In truth, the few moments of this selfsame evening constituted an unimaginable experience which conveyed—Birthed Forth—calm, a peace, and a harmony and to a massive inconceivable degree a flaming love; each attribute appears and diminishes at intervals, until after many years, its effects woefully nearly disappear. By virtue of the knowledge of the experience there remains an elevation of the consciousness of a sustained mode and magnitude, and a gentle considerate demeanor, a contentedness.

Trust in this, one could not predict nor even consider—of the crux—of an event of this nature, afore hand. The merit is as "the smaller fishes being thrown back into the sea in lieu of the one of magnitude" (Paraphrased, obviously). Although in this instance, the smaller fishes are retained as the self-conscious and the one of magnitude is added hereunto. One walks between the raindrops of the material world, while yet living within it.

As a glance, the eternity blossoms within and shines withon the without, as a tiny but radiant light.

Dear Reader, may peace and joy abide with you forever.

## CHAPTER XIV
## Endnote

Endnote 1
*Towards Democracy*, Edward Carpenter. Complete Edition in Four Parts. Published by George Allen and Unwin Limited, at 40 Museum Street, London, W. C., And by S. Clarke Limited, at 41, Granby Row, Manchester, 1916, XLVIII, p 73-74.

**END Part II**

Margaret Mary Stender

# APPENDIX
## —Poetry

Poetry, Enamored of Faraway Heavenly Music

Harken Low to Listen

*"O Prophet heavenly, when I was a little lad asleep in my bed,*
  *and I would close my eyes to pray and question,*
*Then O Prophet, would I open my "head" in belief to listen*
  *—and times, O many times, O heavenly, would I hear,*
*I would hear, a music a-distant a-loft,*
  *and I a-harkening would listen.*

*No distinction would the music make,*
  *all as an orchestra a tuning up,*
*No higher lower sounds, but a harmony, a symphony,*
  *a tuning, a playing distant, faint, just for me,*
*As I a listening, intently concentrating,*
  *not to let the music let away—get away*
*And my intent concentration to get—to hear the music play*
  *sometimes, I could hone to it, find, locate it*
*In the depth within my brain, as I would strain*
  *and hearken low to listen.*

*Then O Prophet, in older years of youth,*
  *the music heard, once heard,*
*Evaded, eluded, my search and never since*
  *was found—have I heard the music*
*—Never returned the music back*
  *so low to listen to harken to hear."*

*"O searching, yearning, longing, soul,*
  *thou hast shadowed over thy music*

## A Tiny But Radiant Light

*With your questioning and doubt and fear,*
*    as with a shadow overcast withholding light*
*    —withshining—from shining*
*Withholding hearing from hearing. O soul,*
*    question not your reasons now for hearing not*

*And harken once again and again low to listen,*
*    break through the doubt and fear,*
*Release the music out once again, again, and*
*    know a-forehand this shall be no easy task,*
*Though the music emburied in you shall also harken low*
*    to listen—to listen for you. Now go in one accord."*
2/17/1996 TGS


Thunderous Sound: The Enkindling—the Crowning;
the crux of this entire narrative, continues with a selection from
*Megan's Story*

*For to sleep in soundness she thought was to accompany her,*
*So to her astonishment she was awakened this time,*
*With the roaring-rage of a Thunderous Storm and winds—On-coming!*
*And fluttering, a whirling, and a pulsing.*
*A rhythm to create within her being and without.*
*The rhythm in synchronization with the sounding of the wings.*

*When the pulsing sounds, with rhythm,*
*Reached their fullest height*
*Of noise and pitch of intensity,*
*An instant flash within her head,*

*A bursting forth a pitch, and pulsing intensity.*
*Megan in astonished recognition knew the feeling, heightened.*
*Then in wonder felt and watched its bursting forth, its ascent,*
*And its descent, slow and slowly through her head it moved,*
*Then to her arms and slowly perceptibly out her arms unto*
*    her hands.*

*Megan felt in bewilderment and questioned it throughout*
*    its travel*

## Margaret Mary Stender

*Through her body, this heightened and slowly moving intimate*
*Awakening the rumble through her body, as it traveled,*
*Slowly, carefully, (as the fear in the days of the Pharaoh),*
*—Eradicating wrong—to the hands and fingers, then it*
*      began again,*
*To move downward in the chest and slowly*
*A full 15-20 seconds, it took to take its journey. Thus*
*It allowed sufficient time to think the thoughts of Megan.*

*Megan can remember thinking,*
*"When this reaches the area of my heart,*
*The fire will burst forth, and with the fire the light,"*
*Immediately thereupon, the traveling stopped, just stopped,*
*Emphatically, abruptly, immediately, and ended,*
*In a line across her chest directly beneath her arms.*

*Megan found herself in crying, she knew in her earthly mind,*
*As it had taken all this time for the circumstance,*
*To be perfect for this event to occur,*
*Then she would never live to see another.*

*Thereupon a crying in rejoicing from the blessedness,*
*And a crying in sorrow mingled for the recognition*
*That it would not likely occur again.*

## Poetry of the Sea of Perpetual Calm

### This Day Awakening Tempering

*To you O morning dawning, I feel the mist a forming,*
*    the numbness, the tranquility on thy brain,*
*The weightiness within mine arms, the heaviness within my chest,*
*    the peace, the calm, forthrighting, bearing down withon*
*      me,*

*Lifting up its voice in spirit, in love in bud, in blossom,*
*    forthcoming, forthgenerating, forthbearing, expelling*
*      itself into the outer sphere,*

## A Tiny But Radiant Light

*To live again unto this day, awakening, tempering all without*
*from within, creating the within withon the without again,*
*again today, today again.*
10/1/1995


## Lull—The Crown of Pearl

*As sitting here, February 7, 2005,*
*in peace unrelenting and tranquility,*
*Having "Heard," again o'er night,*
*though mildly so, the sounding.*
*After days of reading, propounding,*
*after long delay, it occurs,*

*The pinnacle of perfection, Itself, the Lull;*
*ist not forth-worthily expounded.*

*—Nor lauded. I now bow to knee*
*In your venerable presence;*
*To You, O, our perfection.—*

*Herein is the time—promulgating,*
*the Crown of Pearl, the Lull;*
*Make no mistake, the Crown of Pearl,*
*the Lull.*

*The calm, the lull,*
*it is as if time and all eternity*
*stands still.*

*As we walk between the raindrops,*
*nonchalant,*
*unconcerned,*
*in disregard,*
*The height, the breadth, the width,*
*the mind, itself, is occupied upon*

### Margaret Mary Stender

*The peaceful, blissful calm,*
    *permeating, radiating,*
        *substantiating one's body*
      *whole.*

*Not an active though—*
    *a general peace*
        *accompanying one as dew,*
      *the mist.*
          2/7/2005

### Poetry in Light of the Love

### As the Love Doth Live

"And what about Meg, O Lord of hope, of soul?
    Me thinks, I hear you say:"

"Meg is the frailty of things,
    she is the ever young, the gentle,
The hope, turned into faith, transformed to love—Love,
    the substantiality—the fine, the tender powerful,
The strength in tolerance, the understanding in patience.
    (the patience in understanding)
        she is the supple and mallow, she is laughter—the free
          and yielding, the fragrance, color, harmony,
        the giving, the gift giver,

The naive of earthy harsh-eality, the love which ever sees,
    though, sees through faith, feeling, and understanding,
The brain which knows, yet justifies, the tine in time,
    the point, the equal balance, the pinnacle, the
        exactness of the center which stands still,
            —when The Love thus manifests itself
              to her—through her.

## A Tiny But Radiant Light

*Yet, Meg, dost see, perceive, the distancing, the non-committal,*
*    the ever reliant—the knowing, not knowledge*
*        —of the all good,*
*The all for good, underneath, beneath, it all, underlying,*
*    underpinning, undergirding the humanity,*
*        the human-sphere,*
*The material corporal world, the finite, the law of Nature.*
*    She is the advantage of the Eternity under-forcing,*
*Under-supporting, under-shoring, under-stabilizing,*
*    Under-meshing, intermeshing, under-founding,*
*The foundation, the pioneer, the entire whole,*
*    —when, when, The Love dost live in her.*

*She is not the turning, but the*
*    turner of the other cheek,*
*As ye will be—when, as, "The Love*
*    doth live in you."*
        4/3/1997 TGS


## O Gentle Ennoble Man

*O my sweet gentle soul, thou ennoble man,*
*    the heavenly Love doth abide with thee,*
*Doth love thee, engendereth,*
*    and maketh thee whole.*

*Thou doth linger solemn in Its longing,*
*    doth luster in Its joy,*
*Doth pine, with open-wide-stretched arms,*
*    appeal discerningly for Its doting charms.*

*Thou doth glean, doth recline, incline, and lean,*
*    forward into the light*
*Streaming objectively unto, into,*
*    your inner emblazoned sight.*
    —

*Doth Thou know, O Love, his,*
*    —our, receipt ist calm, pure*

## Margaret Mary Stender

*Lulling calm—attending Love,*
    *—Your love from above?*

*Doth Thou know your, Love's effect,*
    *perceive it anon Thyself, in its,*
*In our, reflect, enhanced? Doth Thou feel,*
    *doth Thou share, doth Thou gain too?*
    4/16/2005

## O Gentle Ennoble Man—Expounded

A neutral third party observes and speaks to an individual and also speaks to Humanity as a species.

*O my sweet gentle soul, thou ennoble man,*

The Original Heavenly Love, the Love that exists unto itself, *originates*, in the Eternity, and which is the cause, the birth, the blossom, and the redeemer of the human love, abides with thee.

*    the heavenly Love doth abide with thee,*
*Doth love thee, engendereth,*
*    and maketh thee whole.*

Man inherently longs, lingers, languishes, and pines—knowingly or unknowingly—for his/her eternal Love. When in receipt—as the Love indwells his spirit—the heavenly/eternal Love causes the earthly/human love to glow—a spontaneous glistening Joy, a buoyancy.

*    Thou doth linger solemn in Its longing,*
*        doth luster in Its joy,*
*    Doth pine, with open-wide-stretched arms,*
*        appeal discerningly for Its doting charms.*

Man reaps the proffered harvest generally in proportion to his sincerity, his longing, and his thoughtful and/or prayerful-ardent search. (Though, there are distinct periodic exquisite exceptions, such as in the example of Paul, the Apostle.) Inner light streams into man's inner sight.

## A Tiny But Radiant Light

*Thou doth glean, doth recline, incline, and lean,*
* forward into the light*
*Streaming objectively unto, into,*
* your inner emblazoned sight.*

At this juncture, the third party alters his perspective and directly addresses the eternal Love—the Love Eternal—, Itself, and questions Love's knowledge of Its effect upon his/man's, our, being, when we receive, recognize, or experience Its Presence. The observant and neutral third party then confirms that a silent quieting peace accompanies the Love and rests upon/within Man as a lulling calm. (As a strict aside to this particular poem, the Lulling-Calm causes a distancing, a remoteness, of Man from the material, physical, life and solemnly prompts his desire to enhance his loving search.)

*Doth Thou know, O Love, his,*
* —our, receipt ist calm, pure*
*Lulling calm—attending Love,*
* —Your love from above?*

Do you know, O eternal Love, your effect upon man? Do you perceive in *Yourself,* as we reflect your Love—conjoined with our, with man's, love—back to you? Do you benefit from our love, united with your love, reflected back to you? Do you gain—do you benefit—too?

*Doth Thou know your, Love's, effect,*
* perceive it anon Thyself, in its,*
*In our, reflect, enhanced? Doth Thou feel,*
* doth Thou share, doth Thou gain too?*
4/17/2005


## Furbishing Forth

*"Dear O Prophet heavenly,*
* today I come a test for thee.*

## Margaret Mary Stender

*What, O Prophet heavenly, dost run within the Nature,*
*throughout, without, outside, our door,*
*and never stops evermore?*
*What, O what, dost lie, yet runs, shines with motion,*
*underneath beneath it all?"*

*"Dear Sir, the Selflessness itself flows within the Nature*
*all around and all about, out, without, outside our door.*
*And should we see, and should we be, the example set by Nature,*
*our lives, our life, would be fulfilled in abundance,*
*The abundance in-blossoming for another, and the abundance*
*furbishing for our self, ourselves within."*
10/30/97 TFE

## Poetry in Delight of Vibrant Youth

### O Wondrous Child

*O Lord, the happy child lives within,*
*the happy joyful child, no cares, carefree.*
*The youth, the teasing me, showing he to me,*
*his childhood, his recognition of himself.*

*His power, talents, becoming known to him,*
*displaying to me openly,*
*In various ways amazing*
*—amazing me*
*His generous little pranks*
*—bewildering me.*

*The odds of this occurrence to my finite wondering mind*
*appear beyond the capability of its belief,*
*The winning in the drawings*
*—continually*
*Far beyond my comprehension, my ability.*
*(Even to my wondering finite mind knows*
*it should not be)*

## A Tiny But Radiant Light

*No taking hold, no taking advantage of another*
    *should be, should ever be, not me intentionally,*
*Or me arbitrarily or unknowingly or lovingly, and O*
    *especially by you, O child, O kid, finding your wings.*
*O never let, presume to think, the finite mind*
    *shall be your guidance, conscience, or instructor*
*Never shall it have that aptitude, that attitude,*
    *Yet still, O child, O wondrous child of bliss,*
*We shall not, must not, with your advantage take advantage*
    *of another, not one nor solely any other.*

*O child, O bliss, O happiness,*
    *O wondrous joy, I love thee.*

*Keep thy place, take thy place,*
    *and make my being whole,*
*And shine through me, O loyalty,*
    *to mellow me, O wondrous child,*
*Though, do not take advantage with your*
    *joyful, youthful, toyful, playfulness.*
10/13/1996 TGS


## Yet You Stayed, O Loyalty

O Child, O wondrous child of bliss,
    O wondrous child of happiness,
I knew in my mind, this arrogant finite mind,
    when I wrote this poem, the one above, the poetry
That I should never have presumed to be your guide
    —or guidance and, O child, O wondrous child,
It did not take you very long
    to show me.

Within the hour, within the day, the very same,
    motor trouble, towing trouble, hotel trouble.
Yet you stayed, O loyalty, by my side thus
    all along and saw me through it all.
(Somewhat—with the hours of relaxation
    in the hotel—to my advantage)

# Margaret Mary Stender

*And then the day, the very next, be on our way,*
    *and within the hour, within the day, the very same*
    *—trouble.*
*Within the turns, around the curves, us in serious traffic,*
    *noticed within our ranks a frightful smell*
        *and thought it be a factory.*

*But on we drove for many minutes studying,*
    *until it became excruciatingly clear*
*The fire was within our ranks, undoubtedly*
    *under, right under, the vehicle.*

*And stranded fast in heavy traffic, afraid it would explode,*
    *could not get out, nor to the curb, the freeway so involved,*
*And we began to choke so powerful the fumes. Upon my right,*
    *in desperation, an exit found and pulling off*
*And over, first chance, and immediately*
    *right behind me a slowly burning fire.*

*So into the business office blessed to be right by,*
    *and to the phone and to the fire department,*
*Then of course came the police and a wrecker,*
    *and we, after, many hours awaiting,*
*Rode happily home in the wrecker,*
    *the last sixty miles.*

*And you, O child, remained happy by my side,*
    *though, I was slightly somewhat distraught.*
*And the sun shown from its ebb withon,*
    *withnear, the ground nearby, the horizon*
*The rays of fall showing on the trees,*
    *in brilliant color along the route,*
*The heavily golds and light the yellows,*
    *the radiant reds and mellow greens,*

*And you, O child, O wondrous child,*
    *enjoyed the view and scenery.*
        10/15/1996 TGS

# A Tiny But Radiant Light

## Poetry of the Hallowed Golden Glow

### Withwonderment
### —A Vision

*Last night in deep of darkness still,*
    *the clear, the pure, the sense of silence,*
        *the dark, the night, surrounding,*
            *and you the center of its being,*
*Decided to walk down withon the darkened road*
    *the shiny pavement withunder your feet*
        *within the darkest of dark night.*

*Yet ye can see and clearly so the light within the dark*
    *and ye think to walk, the safety of,*
        *and think again, and look toward your return,*
            *and seeing a pathway as ye turn right,*
                *and noticing, and it drawing*
                      *you toward,*
*Behold a lake withdown the hill,*
    *and the multitude of steps, and you are drawn*
        *and you are drawn, the withwonderment of the lake,*
            *and ye notice suddenly the light, the clear,*
                *the depth within the lake as ye see it*
                    *from the hill, as also from*
                        *the distance,*
*And ye see the golden depth, the space between the surface*
    *within the depth, and ye race toward it,*
        *for the better view from close withon the shore,*

*And ye slide, nearly glide, withover the steps descending,*
    *and ye travel woe to fast, O too fast, and ye miss the view*
        *in depth from withonhigh, and ye slide, and ye glide*
            *withover the surface of the steps,*
                *to withon the shore, and woe is you,*
*The golden, golden, glow, you missed the golden from withon high,*
    *withon the distance, the surface to depth to appear,*
        *(the light from within the depth)*
        *as clear, and pure, enticing, alluring,*
            *the exhibition of its silent self,*

# Margaret Mary Stender

*And ye arrive, and much to thy beholden the wonder of the golden
    depth, still a wonder, yet ye are so very close ye see not
        the panorama from a far and O woe is you,
            you blessed one, the view diminishes.*

            —

*And then you notice and begin to tell the story
    of the golden depth, to unto another, and ye begin to say
        the color, and ye see the mild golden mustard
            of a sweater, and a mellow white olive-green
And ye say, "It is the color of that sweater,"
    then ye think and know unto thyself,
"No wonder, it is the color of the sweater, your eyes
    are resting on, the source is the same,
        and the golden glow is meant for you."*

            —

*And upon your arising, the awakening of your eyes,
    the lids still firmly held in tight,
        you hear the quiet silent flutterings,
            the bare perception of,
                the wings, instilled again,
                      installed again, left again,
                          their silent residue,*

*You feel the gentle silent peace, the gentle quiet calm,
    the silent tone, the calm within.*

            —

*O fellow beings of this earth,
    seek ye within the underneath,
        below the skin, the surface of,
            find and know and explore the love.
The golden glow comes dwells with you,
    from the heavenly above within you.*

            —

*O unto the morning,
    O unto the golden glow,
        the serenity, the humming purring,
            the passive joy, the mirth
                —the merriment*

## A Tiny But Radiant Light

*The silent calm, O remnant of,*
  *O golden glow unto the morning*
    11/22/1996 TGS


## Alight the Night with Daybright

*Dear, O Heavenly, O Heavenly,*
  *come sit and rest awhile with me,*
*Come stand, withover my shoulder to appear, to peer,*
  *to gain the greatest, the vastness, of advantage,*
*To peer, oversee, withover the shoulder of each and all.*
  *The numerous assorted, various, directions, peer.*
*—All within your magnitude, your amplitude, the breadth*
  *of your smile, the congruent consecutive, at once.*

*And steer and guide, direct and lead. Be the pilot, co-pilot,*
  *the navigator, or especially our back-seat driver be, but*
*Be! Be Thyself, Thy Self-appointed, or invited, compatriot,*
  *our confident, our confessor, our helmsman—as Thee are.*
    *(stand staunch in the crow's nest, as Thee do).*

*And understand, (as Thee do), as Thee assuredly do!*
  *and bring us all, the each and all, into, unto one "loop,"*
*One workmanship, the warp and woof, unto the one united whole,*
  *one integrated craftsmanship of congruent continuity.*

*And O Heavenly, while Thee ist about it,*
  *influence our mouth, silence anger, curtail trouble,*
*Ignite the spark, enkindle life—real life—inflame the love,*
  *radiate the joy, the laughter, the inbred youth-like mirth,*
*With adoration, with compassion, with enlightenment and power,*
  *locate the poet, the muse, the kindred soul—each soul.*

*Then watch Thee. Stand Thee back, sit Thee back and watch Thee,*
  *the one, each the person, each community, nation, all,*
*Abound with loving-kindness—alight the night with daybright.*
  *Observe the love, the joy, itself, emerging, glowing forth,*
*As the town within the distant arises, emanates unto the naked eye,*
  *across the bounteous field or plenteous lake in drape of night,*

## Margaret Mary Stender

*The glow—the majestic golden glow*
  *—the radiate, forthward, untoward sky,*
*Untoward heavens, then mingling, commingling,*
    *within the space and beaming streaming on.*
      7/9/1998 TFE

## Then Dawned the Second Birth
## —A Vision

*As on-distant, on-high, from slightly at-left,*
  *he watched as appeared what appeared to be a small mortar,*
*—Transparent, translucent. And within the peripheral vision,*
  *positioned near middle-behind, then shifted to left,*
*Slightly toward left of the mortar, an object, a second.*
  *Though aware of its presence, as transparent and clear,*
  *(abounded by shadows of dusky red.)*

*As accompanied the mortar, never was he to alter his vision to focus*
  *upon it, so engrossed was he in the flare in the mortar.*

*For within the mortar, the broad, thick, shallow, clear mortar,*
  *beheld within his vision, enraptured his attention,*
*A flare, an ultra-glowing, a dazzling, brilliant, luminous, bright.*
  *And as he watched enthralled, the glowing grew,*
*Slowly, perceptively, enlarged and enbrightened.*
  *Then dawned the second birth.*

*A golden radiant glow appeared, radiated slowly, perceptively.*
  *Radiated in its circumference around to surround concentric.*
*Then reached the rim and overflowed. It floated, it flowed,*
  *it glowed. It enhanced its dominion, transformed*
*The tone, the hue, bathed all in golden glow.*
  *It shortened the distance between them,*

*—Till it reached its destination,*
  *the origin of his vision.*
*Then enfolded the glow within,*
  *lighting the Deep-Within-Interior,*

## A Tiny But Radiant Light

*To his knowledge it added,*
*    to the insight, its birth.*

*Tempering. An inner peace, a golden glow,*
*    converged, engulfed, merged, emerged,*
*Transcended him all interior—an interior peace,*
*    an inner glow, surmounting and surrounding him.*
*—*

*He watched the white hot flare as it grew,*
*    as it birthed its golden glow.*
*The golden glow, breathtaking, powerful.*
*    It mellowed, it hallowed, it tarried,*
*Peaceably transforming his perception.*
*    Thus, he perceived the golden glow.*
*        3/24/2000-4/2/2000 Wonderment (W)*

The year 2000 vision of the Golden Glow was so potent in its out-birth, in its origin and effect, in its consequence, that after the poem *Then Dawned the Second Birth* was completed, to assure the vision's comprehension. "It" harried this writer until there caused to bring forth a second poem of even greater stature; further describing the same vision: the hallowed Golden Glow.

## The Golden Hallowed Glow
## —A Vision

*You have heard and seen the story*
*    of the mortar and the pestle.*
*Envision just the mortar,*
*    short and thick and round,*
*With-standing on the ground,*
*    within its inter-midst a glowing white,*
*The ultra-starking bright,*
*    a tiny all-consuming glow.*

*And as he watched enthralled*
*    this within his vision,*
*The ultra-bright, the white,*
*    the piercing light, it grew.*

## Margaret Mary Stender

*It grew so slowly, he watched and he perceived.*
  *It enlarged and grew to slightly within the rim,*
*Then birthed its second glow, the golden glow,*
  *as watched the golden grew, transgressed its parent,*
*Exceeded the circumference of the rim and traveled forth,*
  *slowly enlarging encouraging the perception, to*
  *adhere and to follow.*

*It radiated, it permeated, and shown as sunlight,*
  *thus through the shadow of the trees, doth show*
  *—the golden hallowed glow.*

*Thus as he watched, vision shifted*
  *from the ultra-bright, the starking white,*
*Transfixed, withon the movement of the glow,*
  *as it abounded, it surrounded, the mortar as it grew.*

*Till it reached, its destination, slowly it grew.*
  *It encompassed him, it enlightened him,*
*Until within his inner vision,*
  *he perceived the golden glow.*
*It radiated, it permeated, it caused the sight*
  *within the vision, to change to golden,*
*Mellowing, shimmering, an inner peace,*
  *an inner tranquility, an inner calm.*
*It tallied within his being the peace withon,*
  *—the perceptibly mellowing feeling.*
    3/24/2000-4/2/2000 W


Poetry of the Meant of Creation

All Flaws Abolished by the Light
—A Vision

*The scene the dark of night, yet light,*
  *the mounds of deep and rolling snow,*
*Racing, fleeting, nearly flying down the path,*
  *the trail way of the old railroad track,*

## A Tiny But Radiant Light

*The depth of night, still clearness of perception,*
    *a-lit the way no cause for stumbling to be found,*
*The snow all cleared along the railroad track,*
    *our path ahead prepared and planned for,*

*And she, this women, flighting briskly speeding,*
    *no thought for lack of strength or energy,*
*The gliding, the race, effortless—a gliding*
    *nearly riding racing pacing ahead along the way.*

*One person flighting along behind*
    *merely to her left and several "paces" back.*

*She, in the arms of loving, endearing, night,*
    *peered ahead with beams of light-forth-floating-light*
*Illuminating all the dark, brightening to dusk of night, and*
    *with the light she turned to view, while flighting full ahead,*
*And she espied the source, (as if a tear within the deepest dark of*
    *deepest night, allowing the light full-bursted-light, blare*
        *through) as she turned around semi-somewhat*
*Toward her left, she spied the light far back, yet*
    *toward her right.*

*The light, the full intensity, of blazing, bursting, light,*
    *multiplied and intensified, pure halogen of type*
*And magnitude of white, emerged from-with the point*
    *toward her remote far-back distant right.*

*She turned forward again still flighting in the night, then turned*
    *Again and—had disappeared the ultra-piercing light, though,*
*The source had had its manifestation—She in darkness of the night,*
    *all flaws and deflects abolished, a-banished, by the light,*
*—Still flighting, raising on an incline plane, with-upward*
    *toward the sky, then upward straight without of reach,*
*And with this heightening she felt the mild transition*
    *from the delicate delightful swiftly flighting,*
*To the tingling sensation and the sea of passivity*
    *emerging all around and especially within her.*
*O the stark and glaring light, a-lighting up the night,*
    *and as great, still—as light itself—is its lingering*
*Transfused instilled serenity and blitheful peace and rustic-calm,*

# Margaret Mary Stender

*now manifesting living itself within, generating itself,*
*then reflecting itself without, outside, again.*
3/12/1998 TFE

## Three Landscape Paintings
## —A Vision

*The dreams and so the visions are reappearing,*
*their bounty, their blissful blithefulness,*
*The, somewhat, maze, but always, always, is known*
*the difference from the dream and from the vision.*

*For, again, last night the dreams, a mass, a maze, a haze.*
*Then thus to appear, suddenly startlingly, a gift engifted.*
*The dream of school, of class, of students, one missing,*
*then he returned, sitting beside the side just to the left,*
*And the professor, a generous engifted man, returned,*
*returning the assignments,*

*Gave to all, then gave to me it returned, and as I glanced*
*downward, appeared within my hand, three, yes, I say, three!*
*Beautiful landscapes, simple, eloquent, pastel as green and purple.*
*These three if held together, if placed together*
*One beside the side beside the other, formed, performed,*
*framed, the perfect landscaped painting.*

*Of the wilds of Africa, appeared in simple version to the mind,*
*yet, yet, an animal appeared enmeshed within the one,*
*The rightward one, and this animal, subdued brown in tone, was*
*unfamiliar, but familiar as similar to others we have seen.*

*And I gratefully looked up, the exclamation from the mouth,*
*"Thank you," said me, and he, the professor,*
*Continued on, ignored the "Thank"*
*as nonchalantly as can be.*

*Then looked around to others, they had each and everyone one,*
*three landscape paintings held, and especially,*
*I could see the man onto the left, his three,*

## A Tiny But Radiant Light

*and they compared righteously with mine,*
*And burst then withfrom his mouth, "Thank you,"*
*said he, as the artist continued on.*
　　　　1/21/1998 TFE


## Poetry, the Joy of Immortality

### Sea unto Ourselves

*O me the sea and you the sea in our merging passing,*
*　　abounds the one, the two, the three, conquering*
*　　in our relenting,*
*The sea to be, and you to be, and me to be unto the sea,*
*　　with each and other mindfully recognizing*
*　　and acknowledging,*
*And we the three unto infinity, and each the "other's" equally.*

*So see, sea, unto ourselves, the joy, the freedom of the sea*
*　　a surging mightily, standing unto its own jointfully,*
*　　unitedly, decisively, imploringly,*
*Urging you, urging me, each to be unto the sea, the powerfully*
*　　within, adhering and adjoining, unto the sea, unto the*
*　　liberty, unto immortality, unto eternity, universally,*
*　　and all within the depth the calm within the sea.*

*As when we see the other's view, the view, their view,*
*　　within the sea, we see ourselves less separately,*
*　　the sea to nourish, to flourish all,*
*　　respectfully,*

*As when we see the other's view, the view, their view,*
*　　within the sea, we see ourselves less structurally,*
*　　less importantly, less aggressively, less arrogantly,*
*And view within the view of true, the truth, the freedom*
*　　have attaining,*

## Margaret Mary Stender

*And see within, withon, withfrom, the view perceiving,*
*perceptively, perceptibly, of the sea uniting all,*
*incorporately, cohesively, adhesively, conclusively.*

*O joy of joys!*
    4/17/1996 TGS


## Lull Too

*The aloofness, the distancing,*
*The "no matter"—the indifference.*
*Permeating unrecognized then knowing, merely knowing.*

*Complete thorough recognition—acceptance*
*Silent, unforeseen, inadvertent, unnecessary, acknowledgment,*
*As one becomes a part of it, one Is, and knows!*
*A truth in knowing—the immortality*
*The eternity, everlasting of us—anyway!*
    1/21-22/1996 TGS


## All the While—A Selection

*But behold, just behold, even now, just even now,*
    *the Knowing in "my" mind, ameliorates*
*The earthly circumstance, the earthly attributes,*
    *dis-involves, dis-entangles, the earthly life,*
*And feels and finds the wisdom, the light, thus burgeoning,*
    *swelling, growing, glowing, embrightening, thus inside,*
    10/9/1996 TGS


## Poetry of the Loss of the Sense of Sin

## Goes Its Way a Cautioning

*The conscience seems to be a lonely soul,*
*Has no friendship of its own, no wonder,*
*The temperamental thing, goes its way a cautioning,*

## A Tiny But Radiant Light

*Not once, but twice it calculates, and more,*
*Nearly never abides me to myself, my self, alone,*
*In-twinges itself, in-twines itself, into my being,*
*Into my business, the inquisitive brute, shadowing me,*
*Its finger quaking forward toward my direction,*
*Silently reprimanding, leering at me, prodding me,*

*At some distinction known only to itself alone, relenting,*
*Retreating, to tag, to lag, along behind, to scrutinize,*
*Quietly waiting, patiently observing, enthralled, enticed,*
*Waiting for me to flounder, vigilant, peering, glowering,*
*Scrubbing for every sordid or livid fraction of a detail.*

*Then O then, what does it do, that conscience of mine,*
*After relenting to, and leaving me to my discretion,*
*It sits and whines and sobs and nags, it plagues me, nasty thing,*
*After its "personal" self-relenting blaming me, till I*
*In desperation repent and solemnly, resolvedly, swear*
*And sincerely manifestly promise never to enter into this type*
*Of "contemptible, confrontational, temperamental" behavior again.*

*Is it truly any wonder it has no home, no friend?*
*But why did it choose me to select, elect, befriend?*
*Why am I to be its loyal-ship to? Am I its friend?*
*Am I prime territory? You coward hiding behind me.*
    1/21/1996 TGS


## Macro Goal

*To have one's*
*Conscience*
*So clear that*
*It can not be*
*Found.*
    11/27/1995 TGS

Margaret Mary Stender

Poetry to the Germination or Bud, the Blessed Rhythm

## Ever Faithful

*In my wilting, in my non-caring, caring*
    *in the missing of the one eternal you your long departure*
*Nearly non-my-living, non-existing, in my caring*
    *—not knowing what to do*
*Till I in tired, in predetermined determination,*
    *lay in relaxing and resolve to read my favorite friend*
        *Walt Whitman once again, today all day.*

*And in my caring and in his sharing and in my tired disarray,*
    *I read and read for hours, four hours or more,*
*And placed the book withon my chest and closed my eyes*
    *to rest and did.*

*Then behold, lo and behold, to my wonderment, awakened me again,*
    *to the wings a swishing in their coming—awakening me to*
*Their tone wildly flapping coming closer louder surging bringing,*
    *and in my thinking grateful welcome thankfulness,*
*They blessed me beyond my hopefulness enjoying them,*
    *and in my thinking for awhile just then,*

*The thinking on the palpitation of the wings—their force on me*
    *and compared their presence with—their long pronounced effect*
        *their brushing me—reminded me—their height of joy*
            *—with another satiation in my knowingness!*

*It came in a wave then passed and waved again,*
    *—nearing close, then mellowed in its tone,*
        *and leaving once again*

*Its effects unto my body in my head and ears*
    *reverberated back and back and back,*
        *fluttered back and back and back*

## A Tiny But Radiant Light

*And to my wonderment the memory of the calm adhering,*
*    nor resident in my body, but a remnant, a memory,*
*A "mention" leaving with me—still in this relaxing me,*
*    reminding me, of its faithfulness, though long*
*        in absence faithful, ever faithful lasting.*
*        2/4/1996 TGS*


## From Whooshing Storms to Bearing Life and Calm

*Dear O Heavenly, we search the soul, we search the heart and brain,*
*    and what we see, from this our vantage point, is contrariety,*
*    the hither, yon, the heave and hoa, the love with mirth,*
*        the anger, hate.*

*And as we have spoken thus before, to every thing and obstacle,*
*    an opposite force with it brings—accompanies.*

*For though the one is thus on top, the other sways a-ways beneath,*
*    thus lending in between the two a range, a challenge,*
*    the decisions, the choice of which the way, the direction,*
*    one is, one wills, or is circumstrained to go.*

*And so O Heavenly, here we are age 59 striding water, biding time,*
*    considering, pondering, wondering—knowing some*

*    —a door that opened wide,*
*    —appeasing both the heart and mind:*

*        —the straightforwardness, the eternity known to time,*
*        —the recognition of the plan to right, toward right,*
*        —the happiness, the joyousness—the clinging*
*        permeating unyielding—the blessed unrelenting mirth,*
*        —the fear now long withheld, dispelled-of future,*
*        —the eager anticipation, expectation, of future-*
*        forward, today or within a day, a time, thereafter.*

## Margaret Mary Stender

*And as we sit and as we think, we ponder, wonder, over time,*
  *and see another worrying, solid sunk in deep depression*
  *—(Albeit, 'twas also known to us at one time,*
  *in our near youth, in our near prime).*

*'Tis to him, our friend, we sit and think and ponder,*
  *wonder over time.*

*This too, the contrariety. For a-one seeing clearly, radiant,*
  *and one, another, submerged within the depths,*
  *within the obstacles, the hurdles,*
  *the detriments born with time,*

*And this one, this friend, can not raise his head above,*
  *can not, it seems, see into the future-plus,*
  *the knowingness, pleasantness—the pleasing exhilaration.*

*And how, O Heavenly, do we, do you, afford that one,*
  *that humble, needy, outgoing, altruistic, loving one,*
  *to see the harmony, the symmetry, the grace of peace,*
  *the highlight, the ignition, capable within?*

*This a question born and flown withon the wings of time,*
  *from here this moment launched, re-launched,*
  *from the mystical perspective,*

*And though it knows, it knows not precisely how to attain,*
  *attune, oneself to future-plus, to the eternity*
  *—Known—thus in time.*

*And so unto ourself we know and have in-tried to implant,*
  *in verses various the rhythm—correction! not tried*
  *to implant for that is without of our control.*

  *—The peace, the rhythm of itself implants its character,*
  *its attribute and over time conveys, instills, in-births*
  *within another, as we know first-hand, O Heavenly,*
  *from the blessed-boon Walt Whitman.*

## A Tiny But Radiant Light

*And how can we, presume, even in our knowledge known, advise?*
*    The earth itself, the humanity, itself, has, contains,*
*    The mighty multiple ways and all profess unto their own.*

*Yet this, yea this, is fine, pure-plus, beyond compare,*
*    with any other earthly endeavor, yet known to us,*
*    and constitutes at least one meager step,*
*    one bubble bursting toward the surface,*
*    —farther on and farther known,*
*    than is the general perception.*

*How can we help this friend of ours,*
*    when in ourselves, we have the sparse capability?*
*    We only stand, abide, beside, appeal, or pray, and*
*    offer worldly consolation or effectual suggestion.*

*For this, O Heavenly, is the reason, purpose, of today, to ask,*
*    encourage, for thee thus once again—to bear the wings,*
*    the sounds of surging, racing, whooshing storms of sea,*
*    the lightning strike, the winds, the thunder sounds,*
*    vanishing, diminishing, fading, themselves away,*

*The peace the calm ascending,*
*    the loving listless, the knowledge known,*
*    the eventual glee, the contentedness,*
*    (under what-the-ever-circumstance)*

*—We ask for one, this friend, this day,*
*    we ask for all this day.*

*We do our best yet, yea, best is not enough,*
*    it is Thee, O Heavenly, that possess the key,*
*    that raise the hand held high from ocean's depth,*
*    or depth as sea,*

*That grasp, that clasp, that hand held high*
*    and tug a little—then harder tug,*
*    until the immediacy, the instant stuck,*
*    the lightning strike is passed, is given,*
*    granted, forth, immediate, unrequested,*
*    only fortuitously (grace-given) known.*

## Margaret Mary Stender

*For that is, O Heavenly, is the reason, purpose,*
    *—Love in-dwelled, yet, yea, though bursting forth,*
    *—to ask, encourage, to entreat, to engage, to request,*

*For thee thus once again, to bear the wings,*
    *the sounds of surging, whooshing storms of sea,*
    *the lightning strike, the igniting strike*
    *—changing, charging, bearing life and calm,*
    *—for the one, the friend, and for the every other.*
      6/27/1998 TFE


## ANOTHER'S MYSTICAL EXPERIENCE
### —Non-Poetic

I had previously requested that Samm write a synopsis of his spiritual experience with the fervent intention of placing the description in my *A Tiny but Radiant Light*. Today, I made another request which generated a complete oral delineation of the episode.

He struggled for a moment leaning back in his chair and rubbed his head in a quandary in memory of the difficulty of his childhood and youth and its harsh long term effect. He stated that his memory was a little vague. As he had many times in the past, he first elaborated on the treacheries of his childhood. Only then did Samm blend the effects of his early years with the spiritual enlightenment. This is the entirety of what I wrote immediately after speaking with him. These are the pertinent facts.

Today, July 7, 2008, I went over to my friend Samm's house principally to visit, but also to help him with his flowerpot garden of tomatoes, eggplant, green peppers, and squash. His life story has always been of sincere interest to me as his life has been so severe, specifically: crisis, miracle; crisis, miracle; crisis, miracle; crisis, miracle; crisis, miracle, from start to finish. He, is of interest to me. He is special.

Samm is a man who has lived a life of destiny, growing from a distraught frightened child to a knowledgeable successful

## A Tiny But Radiant Light

personable adult. He is currently eighty-three years old. He lived through, barely lived through, the brutality of a treacherous father, through feeling entirely worthless about himself through all of his years until well after his twenties. He watched his father burn all of his toys, including his precious Hebe.

Hebe was a Raggedy Andy doll. In Samm's own words, "Dad burns up Hebe. All my toys are confiscated, trike, wagon, blocks, and my Raggedy Andy doll that I loved dearly! Andy is not tied to the stake exactly, but he is burned alive as I watch in horror. I was being punished for leaving my stuff scattered on the front porch when a student of my father's came to visit and tripped over the stuff—he didn't fall down or anything, just lost his balance momentarily."

According to Samm, it has only been in the past twenty years that he has begun to secure a hold on his life and has been intensely interested in searching for the *something* greater, or for a purpose, an understanding.

It is not the intention to write of Samm here, as he is able to do that for himself, and has already written about three chapters. Together, we have also tape-recorded the significant parts of his life. However, it is the intention to report on the circumstances leading up to and surrounding his moment of enlightenment.

Undoubtedly, he only entered into the bare twilight as defined by Richard Maurice Bucke; but to some vital degree, he is blessed and has entered in. Yet, the enlightenment was sufficient to enforce a vast impact upon his life; a cause of wonder; a chance to live, to ultimately thrive and grow old.

Samm is certainly blessed: He has been looked-over, guarded over, during the entire period of his life. This is known because he has been safely brought through a multitude of life-threatening events. To name a few: there was the 106-degree fever he suffered as a child, in which the ice man was to leave piles of chipped ice for his mother to place around him on her double bed: he was drastically ill for several days. He was medicated to such a degree that there were times when he did not know where he was. There were many months of recovery. In Samm's words, "At the same time, however, I am knowing that I have always had a special someone, an unseen Somebody, a Steady Hand that sustains me, supports me, comforts me.

"To this day, whenever I stubble and fall (and I still do), and whenever I want to turn and run (and I still do), this someone or Somebody is always there for me to help me back on my feet; to dust me off; to bind up my wounds; to nudge me forward along my chosen way, saying…'Come on Samm, you can do it. I know you can.' The voice is so low, so quiet, and so gentle I have to strain to hear it when it speaks. Believing it, when I've heard it, helps, too. (I'm still learning that one.)"

One of his school teachers tagged him a troublemaker. For instance, he was only capable of drawing airplanes on paper while she was teaching mathematics. His father took away another prized toy, then moved the family into another home and left his precious toy in the loft of the barn. Samm was so terrified of his father that he did not dare to mention to him that it was being left. He knew that he would be in serious trouble if his father knew that Samm saw him place the toy in the barn.

There was the incident where he was forced to run away at about age fifteen, after a severe beating. Only the presence and interaction of his grandmother and mother saved his life. His father had him on the floor kicking him, and according to Samm, "with the distinct intention of killing him." His grandmother and mother pulled the father off and held him until he came to his senses.

There was the incident of being locked in a railroad box car while running away, at age about fifteen, with no water and with the only source of food being fingernails full of beets. The beets were located in the other one-half of the car, restrained by a screen with holes only large enough to allow him to secure mere fingernails of beet at a time. Samm was restrained thus for three days before the boxcar was opened and he was able to jump out.

While running away, he hitchhiked a ride. At one point, he joined a small group of young people who offered him a drink. Later, he awoke and found himself unclothed in the snow, his clothing lying frozen nearby. He was discharged from the Navy with a special discharge, something psychological, as in his words, "They did not know what to do with me." He was incapable of working with others. He described himself as if he were "a meteorite flaring across the sky ready to explode."

His only two friends were his grandmother and mother. He still deemed himself worthless and resisted any suggestion that his mother made to try to encourage him to seek counsel or direction with the church, or by reading the books of inspired men or women.

Samm was twenty seven or twenty eight at the time of the spiritual experience. One day his mother asked him to accompany her in the evening to a mountaintop meeting with amateur astronomers. Generally, Samm always avoided her prompting, especially with respect to anything spiritual. Though, that time, he said that, it was as if he "was of another mind, someone else's mind," and he was eager to accompany her.

After the meeting, he, his wife, and his mother were sitting at his mother's kitchen table. For the first time in his life, he felt refreshed, revived, and to some degree happy. Suddenly, he perceived a lightness, a brightness, a fine ultra-heightened feeling, which he could not understand. Astonished, he repeated over and over. "Don't you feel it. Don't you feel it." His wife felt nothing.

Samm, currently, roughly 55-56 years later, believes that his mother understood what was occurring or, perhaps, to some degree participated in it. (Endnote 1) Everything took place within the confines of one full hour, though he stated that "Time is not valued the same under this circumstance." This condition lasted for about one full year diminishing in a gradual manner from the very first moment. He was more content during this year. It changed his life. He was never the same. Thereafter, he read, went to Unity Church, and desperately tried to enter once again into the bright vibrant existence.

That year he had been selling vacuum cleaners, and felt that it was the only time in his entire life that he was able to achieve or succeed at anything: "school, military, relationships, anything!"

There is no way that I am able to recall all that Samm spoke of today, or especially to relate it in Samm's own personable happy-go-lucky manner or unique style of writing. This all-to-brief overview is set forth—in an altogether non-substantial manner—in an endeavor to record a few meager details until, hopefully, Samm shall bless us with the full detailed description in his own efflorescent words. Only Samm can speak for *only* Samm. (Endnote 2)

His father and mother "are buried to the North of Santa Crux, South of San Francisco, in the virgin redwoods, which are currently burning on this day, July 7, 2008." He has one younger sister living out West, and two younger brothers.

I took two small photos of him with my cell phone, while he was sitting in his chair in front of the non-working computer, relaxing and thoughtfully speaking with me. He is a blessed man. He is my friend.

Upon leaving, Samm said that my visits always energize him. His remark reminds me of Whitman's words from the *Passage to India*, "…thou pleasest me, I thee." 3:08 p.m.

*** 

The above ultra-brief overview of Samm's life and mystical experience was written immediately after I left him and returned to my home, my old Avion, in Batesville, using my notes and my memory of his precise words. In the past, he always prefaced his teenage and adult experiences with details of the severity of his early childhood and its persevering consequence; his disastrous upbringing hung on him like an ironclad cloak for the majority of his years; and, so he did today, as he planned to relate this "life-saving spiritual experience."

If one pays close attention to the above brief narrative, certain aspects of Bucke's marks of cosmic sense are apparent. Samm spoke near endlessly of the hardship and sorrow. The turmoil he was embroiled in during the months and years preceding the mystical experience, corresponds to the desperate struggle of both John Middleton Murry and to me after the death of our loved one. (Endnote 3) In short, the prelude to the experience is thus: he was in complete turmoil for his entire early life; he

## A Tiny But Radiant Light

deemed himself worthless; he was in a continual struggle with life and its realities, he felt completely lost with no apparent relief or recourse to his situation; with no hope.

Consider the following: Bucke's subjective light may be said to have been felt as Samm perceived a lightness, a brightness, a fine ultra-heightened feeling, which he could not understand; for which afterward, he desperately tried to "reenter into," as he described it, "its bright vibrant existence." Bucke's transformation of the subject of the change as seen by others when the cosmic sense is actually present, must have been apparent since Samm, even after all of these years, believed that his mother understood what was occurring or, perhaps, "to some extent participated in it." (This recognition is an essential point.)

Bucke's mark of the suddenness, the instantaneousness of the awakening, definitely occurred with Samm; it occurred unexpectedly with genuine awe accompanying the awareness. With respect to Bucke's mark of cosmic sense, intellectual illumination, Samm was exceedingly interesting and highly intelligent. He was well informed and spoke intelligently on a multitude of subjects; on nearly any subject.

At his death, he owned around two thousand books. (Prior to his death, obviously, I bought roughly thirty of the books which belonged to his mother. They were all spiritual in nature. He loved his mother, Edith, and often spoke of her qualities, and he spoke of his loving grandmother, Nancy, who held him and consoled him, who lived with them.) With respect to Bucke's added charm to the personality, so that men and women are always strongly attracted to the person; Samm had all friends.

During his middle years, he became a gifted photojournalist with photographs appearing in *The Saturday Evening Post* and *LIFE Magazine*. One article titled *The Scene/Horseshoe, Bend, Calif. A Hermit Oblivious of Time and the River* appeared in the September 9, 1966 issue (apparently only the "West Coast" issue), and a photograph appeared in LIFE's Prizewinning Issue, of December 25, 1970, Christmas Day. (Endnote 4)

An afterthought: One more word in commemoration of my friend Samm, and of his integrity and insight gained by virtue of his mystical experience. He struggled for many days in an attempt to write to an old friend concerning a touchy subject. His struggle was over how he, Samm, was to stay within his personal boundaries, and yet encourage his friend to forgive another person for a nearly intolerable injustice. He did not know how to put it into words without causing another type of intrusive hurt. In a quandary, and after fretting over the situation for many weeks and mentioning it to me on several occasions, he finally completed a nine page heartfelt letter; the first seven pages were full of grand memories.

My intention is to quote a tiny portion which appeared near the end of the letter from a copy which Samm gave to me:

"Okay. But enough of this: It has now come to 'put up or shut up' time. We are now—finally—where the rubber meets that hard road. So, here goes; ready or not. Ever since learning (a little over a month ago) that you might soon be 'outward bound,' I have had this urging this knowing, that there is something I need to share with you. A 'message.'

"…Seeing as how it is that one of 'the rules' in this electromagnetic universe we live in is that the more we push against something the more it pushes back. And the more we try, for example, not to think of something, the more we end up thinking about it. Most importantly of all, the more we try to free ourselves from whatever it is that holds us, the firmer its grip. The bottom line, so called, is that we—none of us—have either the power or the right to make anyone a non-person. Whatever the provocation! Not without reducing ourselves in the attempt, at any rate. Carry all of this out far enough and it makes for some very heavy luggage. Too heavy to lift, much less carry. Especially in the case of someone wanting to visit those bright lights in the heavenlies. The air is pretty thin and fine up there. So I'm told.

"So…what to do? And, how to do it. A question I hope and pray you will ponder and contemplate between now and
departure time. This is serious soul food we're into here old friend. So please stay with me and hear me out.

## A Tiny But Radiant Light

"The thought here is that you will do well to consider a possibility you're likely never so much as imagined before, much less considered actually doing. According to this wee small voice of mine, somehow, some way, you need to find a way to forgive _____. Across-the-board. Unconditionally. No strings. No ifs. No ands. No buts.

"Why in God's name would I need or want to do that?!? I'm sure you're explaining right about here. The short answer is... Because 'To err is human. To forgive is divine.' And, because sooner or later, you will end up forgiving _____ anyway. Because sooner or later you must. That, too, is one of The Rules. But more importantly, perhaps, at least for right now, because *it will feel ever so good when you do!* And there is nothing, here or in the hereafter, more wonderful than feeling good. As in complete. As in whole.

"It might make things a bit easier for you to realize that none of this has anything to do with right vs not right, good vs not good, deserving vs undeserving. It's not one of those 'this-or-that' kind of things. It also has nothing to do with _____, not directly at any rate. But, the bottom line is that if you can somehow, some way, find a way to pull this off, it will do you (yourself) a world of good! And, guess what else? It will be good for all of everything. Good for the butterfly on the blossom, and good for the bullfrog in the pond. Even the stars in the sky will twinkle just a tiny bit brighter. All because my friend went home in peace instead of at war. How do I know all this is so? I don't! But that wee small voice knows. As for my personal self, all I know is that I need to learn to trust it, and follow its guidance. But there is no explaining it, and no telling it in words. ...Just be knowing, and *believing*, that when we forgive, everyone and everything is blessed. Including heaven itself.

Once again: You are not doing this for anyone except my ol' friend himself. This is all about **your** journey. If you want to go where the lights are extra bright, ya gotta travel extra light. You won't even need a comb or a toothbrush, much less any anger, grief, or sadness to weigh you down in the heavenlies. So, I will be praying for you to free yourself of all that 'feel bad' stuff, and instead reach for joy, and play a happy tune. If you can do that, happy dancers will join you, in the here and the now, and in the hereafter."

\*\*\*

Eight days before his death, I noted in my journal: Tonight, Samm in the hospital, with his legs dangling over the edge of the bed, and with a twinkle in his eye, informed me that, ...yet, somehow, there remained a spark deep within where he knew that he was not a lost soul, not a worthless being, not without purpose. He said that he "knew that he knew," did not "believe," but with emphasis, he said that he "knew" that he was set apart. Having said that, he also said"...that anyone that said that they knew rather than believed was also looked-at askance by other individuals."

"...Knew that he knew..." Samm had just used my language. His comment reinforced my "knowing," my Knowledge Known. I could not help but notice.

# APPENDIX
## —Endnotes

Endnote 1
Samm noted that his mother also had a spiritual experience. Samm does not recall the magnitude of the experience, "but it allowed her to carve out a space or territory of her own" wherein "she was able to live." She had also been under a severe hand.

Endnote 2
Samm was born September 8, 1924 and died on January 30, 2010, before completing the story of his life.

Endnote 3
It also corresponds to the shock of the loss of John Middleton Murry's boyhood friend, by lightning strike.

Endnote 4
On September 20, 2000, in a letter to a friend, Samm wrote of one of his photos, "...The subject of which is a picture that once rated centerfold position in Life Magazine's All Photography Issue. A somewhat youngish happy couple with their four very photogenic children. They're posed (I took the picture originally for them to send back to the Netherlands as a Christmas card) on, in, and around, this great looking old Model A Ford pickup truck, with a couple of sacks of ready mix concrete on the running board. The time was mid-60s. The place was the fabled (then and now) Mendicino County on the northern California coast. This picture has been reproduced several times, including the Time Life book Joy of Life, and the ultra-slick magazine the U.S.A. used to print and distribute in the U.S.S.R. It also made the pages of France's leading magazine, The Paris Match."

**End: A Tiny but Radiant Light**

Made in the USA
Monee, IL
09 September 2021